MORE
Secret Stories of
Walt Disney World

More Things You Never Knew
You Never Knew

Jim Korkis

Foreword by Werner Weiss

Theme Park Press
www.ThemeParkPress.com

Editor: Bob McLain
Layout: Artisanal Text

ISBN 978-1-68390-022-1
Printed in the United States of America

Theme Park Press | www.ThemeParkPress.com
Address queries to bob@themeparkpress.com

Dedicated to Michael Shawn and Laurel Slater, who met and fell in love when they were the last two finalists in a "sudden death" overtime round during a cast member Walt Disney World trivia competition.
They later married and had two sons and created their own Disney history.

In the 1990s, Shawn worked as a show writer for Walt Disney World Imagineering and he and his wife gave presentations and park tours to cast members to share the true stories of Walt Disney World.

In March 2009, Shawn set up a website sharing some of those same stories. This dedication is to thank them both for keeping the stories alive..

Other Books by Jim Korkis, from Theme Park Press:

The Vault of Walt: Volume 5 (2016)

The Unofficial Disneyland 1955 Companion (2016)

How to Be a Disney Historian (2016)

Secret Stories of Walt Disney World (2015)

The Vault of Walt: Volume 4 (2015)

The Everything I Know I Learned from Disney Animated Features (2015)

The Vault of Walt: Volume 3 (2014)

Animation Anecdotes (2014)

Who's the Leader of the Club? Walt Disney's Leadership Lessons (2014)

The Book of Mouse (2013)

The Vault of Walt: Volume 2 (2013)

Who's Afraid of the Song of the South? (2012)

The Revised Vault of Walt (2012)

Contents

Foreword

February 8, 2008, was one of those perfect days at Walt Disney World. The temperature was around 80 degrees, with a breeze keeping things comfortable. But what really made it perfect was walking around World Showcase Lagoon at Epcot with Jim Korkis.

At that time, Jim worked at the Epcot Learning Center, an educational resource for Disney cast members. Jim and I had been reading each other's online articles for quite some time and had occasionally traded emails, but we had never met in person. Although our time was limited to Jim's lunch period, we made the whole loop of the lagoon, stopping at the old Yakitori House for lunch and at the American Adventure lobby to listen to the Voices of Liberty.

As we passed the countries of World Showcase, Jim pointed out details that lend authenticity to each of the pavilions, even though guests seldom know their significance. He mentioned plans proposed for the areas that were never built. Jim wasn't reciting trivia or statistics. He offered genuine insight that would increase a guest's appreciation of the park.

When I read the first volume of *Secret Stories of Walt Disney World*, I was reminded of that day at Epcot with Jim. Once again, Jim made Walt Disney World a more interesting place.

Jim has spent a lifetime collecting historical details about Disney parks, Disney animation, Disney live action, Disney merchandise, Disney publications, the talented people who created them, and the life of the genius who started it all, Walt Disney.

He has absorbed this information from many sources, including directly from the people responsible. Perhaps Jim doesn't know everything about Disney, but that's not from lack of trying. There might not be anyone who knows more about such a wide variety of Disney topics.

Jim is generous with his knowledge. His articles and books are a reflection of who he is. As a columnist, author of books, and speaker, Jim shares stories about all things Disney with appreciative audiences.

It's not just the quantity of Jim's knowledge; it's also the quality. Jim knows the difference between real back stories and the myths that only seem real. Jim knows the historical context that gives meaning to how things are today. And Jim knows the stories beyond the carefully crafted corporate Disney versions.

Since we first met at Epcot, Jim and I have walked around other parts of Walt Disney World. Somehow, we haven't yet made it to Disney's Animal Kingdom together. (Hey Jim, when can we change that?)

As you read this book, think of it as walking all over Walt Disney World with Jim. You'll find yourself in corners you never knew about. Sometimes, you'll travel back in time. You'll meet some of the people who created the "World". You'll experience places that never escaped from the planning process. And you'll see familiar spots in a new way.

In this book, Jim gives you succinct, fun-to-read, two-page articles. There are far more secrets than you would get from a week of walking around with Jim. And you don't even have to bring an umbrella in case it's not such a perfect Florida day.

Werner Weiss
July 2016

Werner Weiss is the "curator" of Yesterland.com, a theme park history website launched in 1995. Originally focused on discontinued Disneyland rides, shows, parades, and restaurants, the site has expanded to include Walt Disney World, other themed entertainment, and even Disney myths. He is a recognized Disney authority and for decades readers have enjoyed his evocative writing and historical photos.

Introduction

In these days of the internet, there are so many sites devoted to Walt Disney World that few things are really secret to the diligent fan with plenty of time to explore. The Disney Company is deeply concerned that these people are able to discover detailed information about changes at Walt Disney World before Disney is ready to officially announce them.

However, there are just as many, if not more, fans and even cast members out there who are unaware of most of these sources but still love knowing more about the stories behind the stories. They are interested not just in the newest additions but the stories behind them as well as the stories behind the things that they have enjoyed for years or that have disappeared over time.

Unfortunately, over the last forty-five years, many of the stories about Walt Disney World have become a muddle of half-truths, obfuscations, marketing malarkey, and outright falsehoods.

Repetition of these familiar stories that "everyone knows" introduces unsuspecting new generations to the same Disney myths and misunderstandings. The internet can be a good source of information but only if you know what information to completely ignore because it is sometimes merely opinion, conjecture, or simply a repetition of false information without attribution.

Unfortunately, the Disney Company was never too diligent in recording the background information about Walt Disney World. It is not always trustworthy to depend just upon the memories of those who experienced something at WDW because what is remembered has been forever altered, sometimes slightly and sometimes drastically, by the filters of subjectivity, self-interest, and emotion.

This book tries to offer a more accurate accounting of the actual stories even with the constant changes happening at Walt Disney World. Elements of the parks are constantly and quietly disappearing piece by piece, often with no advance warning or announcement. If we don't start documenting this material, one day that background information will be gone forever along with some favorite treasure that vanished between vacation trips.

One of the things that make a Disney theme park a different experience is that it tells stories that link with other things to create an overall immersive narrative. When newly installed CEO Michael Eisner was introduced to this concept by Imagineering, he coined the term "Everything Speaks" meaning that everything in the park should have a story.

That was never Walt Disney's intention. He never meant for everything to have its own individual story but that it should all help contribute to telling the same story and not contradict that story. Some things like trash cans were merely necessary and functional but were designed to reinforce the overall theme of an area with decorations relating to a specific land.

Sometimes a popcorn cart is just a popcorn cart.

Mr. Mulligan, a local farmer, had a season where he harvested an exceptionally large crop of corn. It was so much that it spilled out of the silo into the nearby barn where Mulligan had a large collection of wagons that he used to rent to neighbors.

He had purchased the famous cow from Chicago's Mrs. O'Leary, a distant relative, and one night the bovine again carelessly knocked over a lighted lantern and the barn caught on fire. It was so hot that the kernels of corn popped and the wagons in the barn were filled with popcorn before the flames could be extinguished.

A desperate Mulligan drove his wagons, now filled to overflowing with hot popcorn, to the market where he sold bags of the treat to recoup some of his financial losses and get rid of the damaged corn. The activity was so popular that Mulligan repeated it the next year and several years following and this tradition is represented by the popcorn cart at the front of Main Street, USA

Is that a true Walt Disney Imagineering back story?

Well, it's true that it is a story, but, no, it is merely a fanciful anecdote I just created on the keyboard. It *seems* to makes sense with the elaborateness of detail giving it more credibility.

WDW cast members do the same sort of thing all the time to fill in the vacuum of not knowing the real story.

Imagineering even has a term for this type of story invention created by cast members and guests: "logical erroneous conclusion".

Basically, the term refers to adding two and two together and getting five or seven or something other than the real answer. It seems to make sense from observation or imagination, but it has no basis in what was actually intended.

For instance, the architectural structures on top of WDW's Haunted Mansion are not chess pieces even though they might remotely resemble them.

In the early days of Eisner's management to reinforce his "Everything Speaks" concept, Imagineers were encouraged to create convoluted backgrounds for the simplest of things, from a new cart serving early morning coffee in the lobby of the Wilderness Lodge to a broken-wheeled wagon in Frontierland selling French fries.

Disney Archivist Dave Smith actually stopped collecting those tales because they didn't seem to come intrinsically from the item but were just awkwardly overlaid and were often too excessive and long-winded.

Neither guests nor cast members understood or accepted that the Rock'n'Roller Coaster attraction was in 1940s Hollywood because it was actually a popular recording studio in the 1930s that closed because of the disaster at the Hollywood Tower Hotel in 1939. It struggled for many years to survive its "bad omen" reputation associated with that incident but finally re-opened.

It never seemed to bother guests that it was there at all nor occur to them that it exists where it is today simply because that is where land was available to build and operations needed some other attraction to handle the crowds being drawn down to the dead end Sunset Boulevard.

Often times, even in Walt's era, decisions about the park were based on finances and not necessarily storytelling. Adventureland got moved to a different location than originally planned because there were existing trees in an area and that would cut the costs of landscaping.

Drunk partiers at Pleasure Island had no interest spending their evenings in learning the complicated story of Merriweather Adam Pleasure by reading the many plaques installed outside of the nightclubs. As venues closed and were replaced by other entertainments, it became even more complicated to try to integrate the new additions into that muddled storyline.

Disney needn't have tried to bother because guests didn't care. Guests may care about some obvious contradictions like a spaceman walking through Frontierland, but many other things are just not important enough to be on their radar.

Cast members have created a faux atmosphere in some areas because they were never trained about the intended story. During Walt's era, standard operating procedure handbooks included the historical and story background of the attraction. The one for the operation of the Submarine Voyage had a lengthy introduction written by Admiral Joe Fowler himself.

To save money and try to prevent possible future legal issues that cast members were not following approved procedures, those training manuals no longer physically exist.

So, cast members at Twilight Zone Tower of Terror act as if they are dead which irritates Imagineers constantly. An Imagineer responsible for the attraction told me:

> The host and hostesses at the Haunted Mansion are dead. They are part of the ghosts that inhabit the building. At the Tower, they are trapped in time and space, another dimension of time and space like the Twilight Zone itself. They are trapped in 1939 so the eerie thing is that they act as if it is 1939 at the time of the accident and treat you as if you were a guest coming to stay at the hotel. That is what is supposed to make them scary.

When I asked him why he didn't simply go over and tell the cast members, he replied, "They have to pay for that now." Once Eisner became CEO, he insisted that every department show a double-digit percentage profit each year, even Imagineering.

So how does something like maintenance show a profit since it is not selling anything? By eliminating hours or staff. How did Imagineering show a profit? By shredding material they had in storage to save insurance and storage costs, especially for items that were never built like the Matterhorn attraction proposed for World Showcase or things that were removed because it was felt that information was no longer necessary.

Only items relating to currently operating buildings needed to be saved and even in those cases perhaps only the paint chips in order to recreate the proper color rather than the documentation of why certain things were there.

I saw it happen when the Disney Institute closed its physical location and was replaced by the Saratoga Springs Resort.

Things like early concept sketches, curriculum guides, documentation video tapes of presentations done in the Cinema and Performance Center, and other items were tossed haphazardly into a dumpster and cast members were warned that it was an immediate dismissal offense to remove anything because it was Disney property.

So, the wonderful two-hour show by film restoration expert Scott McQueen talking about animated projects Disney never made and showing examples of some of them that he found mislabeled in storage was destroyed.

The huge book kept by the Animation Department with original artwork by visitors like Ward Kimball, Marc and Alice Davis, and John Canemaker was vandalized and the surviving artwork thrown away.

It was simply not cost effective for the Disney Company to treasure all its heritage and the Disney Archives always had only a tiny budget and limited storage space to preserve the most important things, with priority always given to items from the West Coast.

In addition, to show that it was a revenue-generating division, Imagineering began charging an exorbitant hourly rate to talk with an attraction area. That rate included time for research, preparation, visual materials, travel, the actual presentation itself, and in some case, compensation for the "lost" work time of the Imagineer on that particular day. It became quite expensive.

Two years ago, I asked a question at Guest Relations at the Magic Kingdom in Florida about the exact length of Main Street, USA. They spent over an hour looking and couldn't find the answer. I asked if they might phone someone at Imagineering to find out. They replied that they would have to pay Imagineering for the answer and it might take days for a response and that since I was the only person who had ever asked that question, they couldn't justify the cost of asking.

What I hope makes this book different from all the others that are out there is that I worked at Walt Disney World in a variety of different departments, had access to company libraries (some of which no longer exist), interviewed Imagineers and original cast members, and one of my roles was to share Disney heritage in over 250 different presentations and tours that I researched, wrote, and presented not just to cast members but to many of Disney's corporate partners like Kodak.

It never occurred to me that one day I might be among the last men standing that actually knew certain information. Some of that knowledge was considered commonplace and others knew it as well. That is not the case today, as so many people have passed away, left the company, or been laid off.

In addition, I am sharing these "secrets" differently. They are not just a short paragraph of trivia but a two-page story filled with quotes, measurements, facts from official documents, and descriptions. All of this information is greatly distilled from much larger and verified source articles I have written over the decades.

As I tell people, no one can know everything...especially about Disney. I am constantly learning, and many things I thought I knew, I will discover that I didn't understand the whole story as new material is uncovered.

It is hard to find these stories and even harder to verify them from multiple other sources. Sometimes Disney no longer has the information. Sometimes Disney has quarantined the necessary information so it is unavailable to outside researchers or even interested cast members. Sometimes Disney never had the information in the first place.

The Disney company was always a company of oral history, passed along but not written down by the people who worked on a particular project because there was always so much pressure to get work done. Once a project was completed, there was the rush to get to work on the next project which was always somehow already behind schedule.

One of the nicest compliments I ever received was from a young lady who wrote to me and said that what she enjoyed most about my writing is that she felt smarter after reading it. I hope there are others who feel the same way.

Walt Disney World always seems to be the neglected "orphan child" when it comes to books telling that history. Everyone wants to write about Disneyland which has its own intimate charm and often childhood connections.

When I started to work at Walt Disney World, I learned more about the vacation kingdom and began to appreciate it in a much different way. For some people, it is their first connection with a Disney theme park and it has its own unique history needing to be shared.

This book and the previous volume are a good start, but there are so many other stories that were unable to be included for a variety of reasons. I hope you enjoy the tales on the following pages. I hope they encourage you to search for additional information as well as enhance your appreciation of Walt Disney World.

Jim Korkis
June 2016

PART ONE

The Walt Disney World Parks

The Themed Entertainment Association (TEA), an international non-profit organization devoted to the themed entertainment industry, released its estimated theme park attendance report for 2015. Theme parks do not report their attendance publicly and, in fact, Disney announced a slight decline at all its theme parks during 2015, perhaps because even though attendance increased, it fell below projections.

Overall, in 2015 Walt Disney theme parks saw a growth of 2.7%, enough to keep it at number one in theme parks and amusements worldwide. Even with nearly a 12% overall growth overall, Universal theme parks still remain a distant third. The top 10 global theme parks by attendance in 2015 (by millions of visitors) were:

1. Magic Kingdom: 20.5, 6.0% (growth rate)
2. Disneyland: 18.3, 9.0%
3. Tokyo Disneyland: 16.6, -4.0%
4. Universal Studios Japan: 13.9, 17.8%
5. Tokyo Disney Sea: 13.6, -3.5%
6. Epcot: 11.8, 3.0%
7. Disney's Animal Kingdom: 10.9, 5.0%
8. Disney's Hollywood Studios: 10.8, 5.0%
9. Disneyland Paris: 10.4, 4.2%
10. Universal Studios Florida 9.5, 16.0%

Apart from its usual role as a "vacation kingdom", Walt Disney World is an environmentally responsible corporation and an integral participant in the economic well-being of central Florida:

- Nearly one-third of Walt Disney World's property has been set aside as a dedicated wildlife conservation area.

- On an average day, there are approximately 250,000 people on Walt Disney World Resort property, including cast members, other non-Disney employees, and guests.

- Disney is the largest single-site employer in the United States, employing approximately 74,000 cast members in central Florida, in more than 3,000 different job classifications with total 2015 annual payroll of $2.4 billion. WDW is the largest single taxpayer in Central Florida, contributing $601 million in total state and local taxes paid and collected for 2015.

- Walt Disney World cast members come from all over the world, representing more than 80 nationalities and speaking more than 50 different languages.

- WDW contributes to the community through cash donations and in-kind support for local nonprofit organizations and hundreds of thousands of volunteer hours by Disney cast members through a company organization called VoluntEARS. In 2015, Disney hosted more than 7,500 wish trips for children and donated tickets valued at more than $14 million to Give Kids the World Village and other wish-granting organizations.

- Disney Harvest reduces food waste by gathering excess prepared food from Walt Disney World resort kitchens, more than 820,000 pounds of it, and distributing it through the Second Harvest Food Bank of central Florida. The Disney Harvest Program celebrated its 23rd year in 2015.

- WDW works to reduce energy consumption, increase use of reclaimed water, and implement diversion of waste from landfills.

- Disney's Animal Programs teams at Disney's Animal Kingdom and Epcot's The Seas with Nemo and Friends are devoted to the care of more than 7,000 birds, mammals, reptiles, amphibians, fish, and insects, including 35 endangered and threatened species. Both facilities are accredited by the Association of Zoos and Aquariums (AZA). As part of the AZA Species Survival Plans that focus on cooperative breeding and management groups for critical species, Disney's Animal Programs has successfully bred endangered species like African elephants and black rhinos.

All Aboard the WDW Railroad!

At Walt Disney World, guests enjoy an approximately twenty-minute journey over one and a half miles of track surrounding the park on one of four meticulously restored, working narrow-gauge trains originally built between 1916 and 1928.

There are views of things that can only be seen from the train, like a glimpse inside Splash Mountain and a more leisurely look at the flooded town of Tumbleweed at Big Thunder Mountain.

The railroad serves two purposes. First, it is transportation to access the extremities of the park. Second, its original intent was to provide guests with a comfortable overview of the layout of the Magic Kingdom, a "grand tour", which is why when the park opened in 1971 there was only one train station at the entrance to the park on Main Street, USA, inspired by an actual turn-of-the-century Victorian station in Saratoga Springs, New York.

In May 1972, a small one-room train station with benches opened in Frontierland just northwest of the Pecos Bill Café. Located there was the water tower necessary to service the trains. The station closed in November 1990 to accommodate the building of Splash Mountain and was relocated and reopened in December 1991.

"When we started talking about trains for Florida, I pointed out that it would be better to find equipment in existence than to go through building everything from scratch," said Imagineer Roger Broggie who went to Mexico to check out four narrow-gauge steam engines.

During the late 1960s, the Mexican government was converting its railway system to diesel-electric locomotives and was in the process of retiring the old Baldwin locomotives (built in Philadelphia) that had hauled sugar cane, bales of sisal fiber, and other items on the Yucatan Pennisula.

The Mexican officials accepted eight thousand dollars each for the four engines selected. The engines were rechristened the Walter E.

Disney, Roger E. Broggie, Lilly Belle (to honor Walt's wife Lillian), and Roy O. Disney.

Amusingly, Broggie noticed a pile of discarded vintage brass bells, whistles, light housings, and other fittings, and tentatively asked what the Mexicans intended to do with these items. He was happily surprised when told he could take whatever he wanted for free. He filled up half a boxcar with the fittings and spare parts.

Broggie had selected the Tampa Ship Repair & Dry Dock Company in Tampa, Florida, to do the restoration on the engines. The factory had never worked on trains before. They specialized in converting large freighters into oil tankers. However, the Disney company wanted to build a strong relationship with local Florida businesses, and that was one of the reasons the choice was made.

The boilers were replaced by new ones from the Dixon Boiler Works of Los Angeles. Other repairs and refurbishments, such as the replacement of rotting wood, were also made. All the work was finished in roughly two years.

The passenger cars were fabricated from scratch in the same warehouse where the locomotives were renovated.

The Swing Bridge is located just north of Big Thunder Mountain, spanning a canal that connects the Rivers of America to the Seven Seas Lagoon. It is called a swing bridge because it pivots, or swings, on a center support, allowing boat traffic to travel through the waterways to the dry dock backstage.

The bridge is actually a piece of "Old Florida" and was originally part of the Wabasso Bridge running over the Indian River near Vero Beach until the entire bridge was updated shortly before Walt Disney World was built.

In the rush to ride all the thrill attractions at the Magic Kingdom, it is nice that one of the oldest traditional experiences still exists for guests to enjoy with no need for using MyMagic+ to schedule an unforgettable experience.

Cosmic Ray's Starlight Café and Sonny Eclipse

Cosmic Ray's Starlight Café, a popular chain of intergalactic food and beverage franchises with a "galaxy of food choices", has been open for business in Tomorrowland since 1994.

The restaurant was previously called the Tomorrowland Terrace, until 1994. The original performer for the first decade was Michael Iseberg (aka Michael Iceberg) who amazed audiences with his frenetic performances using his early keyboard and synthesizer technology on his Amazing Iceberg Machine.

"This is the FIRST Earth Restaurant Franchise from Outer Space" proclaimed the original poster for what was the largest quick serve location at the Magic Kingdom with its three food bays and extensive topping bar.

Guests dining in the Starlight Lounge Room on the lower level near the Alice in Wonderland tea cup attraction enjoyed the song stylings and snappy banter of audio-animatronics lounge performer Sonny Eclipse (voiced by blues singer and songwriter Kal David) during his approximately twenty-plus minute performance.

Sonny was modified from a similar figure, Officer Zzzzyxxx, who was at the baggage screening desk outside of the Star Tours attraction at Tokyo Disneyland. Today, Disney refers to them as "cousins".

Direct from Yew Nork on the planet Zork, Sonny Eclipse is the "Biggest Little Star in the Galaxy", according to his billing. The Bossa Supernova and Eclipso musical stylings of Sonny and his Astro Organ, along with his ethereal and invisible backup singers The Space Angels, have entertained guests for over two decades. His unseen technician is named Mike Feedback.

During his act, Sonny mentions his six-eyed (all purple), twelve-nostrilled girlfriend who blows him away, and he sings a little love song he wrote for her entitled "Oh Bright Little Star". His jokes, always followed by canned laughter, include such groaners as:

> Hey, speaking of planets, Donald Duck and Goofy were in here a few minutes ago looking for Pluto. Man, are they a few million miles off, or what?

The Metrophone booth from the Galactic Communications Network (GCN) located near the Tomorrowland Transit Authority PeopleMover connects guests to nine possible hilarious one-sided conversations including one with Johnny Jupiter, Sonny's agent.

Kal David had been working in Los Angeles with George Wilkins, who wrote a great deal of music for Disney. Wilkins brought David in to sing the song "Unhealthy Living Blues" for the Goofy About Health section in Epcot's Wonders of Life Pavilion in 1989. It went so well that he brought David back to perform as the voice of Sonny Eclipse.

It was all done out of Wilkins' southern California home where he had set up a studio. Wilkins did all of the music on his synthesizer except for the guitar parts that were done by David, who was even able to incorporate a little of his famous blues guitar style in the song "Gravity".

David worked for about three days. His female backup singers were The Brunettes, a group that featured David's wife Lauri Bono who still tours with him today. The women worked for one day and were crammed into a small vocal booth that included Wilkins' washer and dryer. One of the singers, Amy, was pregnant at the time. David recalled:

> Everything was all written for me. There was no ad-libbing. It was just another short studio gig and then you went back to your real life. They showed me a drawing of the character and encouraged me to just be myself. I loved him immediately and I had played in many bars over my career so I understood the 'feel' of how he would be.
>
> I could have done a cartoony voice but they just wanted my real voice pumped up a little. I like the songs but they are not the blues. I am proud to be the voice of Sonny. It has turned out to be the steadiest performing gig I ever had.

McDonald's in Frontierland

McDonald's executive Ray Kroc wrote the following letter to Walt Disney on October 20, 1954:

> Dear Walt, I feel somewhat presumptuous addressing you in this way yet I feel sure you would not want me to address you any other way. My name is Ray A. Kroc. ... I look over the Company A picture we had taken at Sound Beach, Conn., many times and recall a lot of pleasant memories. ... I have very recently taken over the national franchise of the McDonald's system. I would like to inquire if there may be an opportunity for a McDonald's in your Disneyland Development.

A young Walt Disney was assigned to the American Red Cross Ambulance Corps unit training in Sound Beach in 1918 and eventually went to France even after the Armistice officially ended World War I. Kroc was also in that unit but did not go to France.

Walt responded with a warm letter informing Kroc that his request had been sent to C.V. Wood in charge of Disneyland concessions because things were too hectic at the moment for him to handle it personally. Kroc claimed he never received a response from Wood.

McDonald's did get a presence in Disney theme parks due to an agreement with Disney from 1997 to 2007.

The McDonald's Fry Cart that opened in 1999 was located near Pecos Bill's Tall Tale Inn and Café and sold its famous French fries and soft drinks. Disney Imagineers wrote the following back story for that location:

> With the rush of prospectors passing through Frontierland in search of gold, lots of folks in town started looking for ways to cash in on all the excitement. Back in 1853, ol' McDonald (who had a farm, "ei-ei-o"), a potato farmer, decided to set up his cook wagon on the hill under the big oak tree, just off the main trail.
>
> To drum up interest in his French fried delicacies, McDonald even came up with a catch phrase and posted it on the front of the wagon:

"There's gold in them thar fries!" (with a symbol of a golden arch to emphasize the fact).

Business was booming for a couple of good years, right up until the great flood of 1855. Legend has it that white men disturbed the spirits of the mountain by removing gold from Big Thunder, causing all sorts of havoc, from earthquakes and avalanches to storms and floods.

In fact, the nearby river rose so much, the water reached right up to McDonald's wagon on the hill. The wagon survived, but when the water receded, the wagon started to go with it. It slid down the hill, crashed through a fence (and sharp-eyed guests could see the poorly repaired fence and a broken wagon wheel), and got lodged in the mud down below.

This didn't stop ol' man McDonald, though. He just laid down some planks so folks wouldn't get their boots muddy, and he has kept right on selling his delicious French-fried potatoes until the Disney agreement ended.

There was also a sign placed nearby that proclaimed, "Same location since '53." The "53" was scratched out and painted over with a "55". Not only did this help support the story that the wagon had moved, it was also a reference to McDonald's history.

Brothers Dick and Mac McDonald opened their original restaurant in San Bernardino, California, in 1953. Kroc, who pitched the idea to the brothers of expanding their restaurant into a franchise, opened his first location in Des Plaines, Illinois, in 1955.

The Frontierland Fry Cart closed in December 2007. Just over a year later, on January 11, 2009, the Golden Oak Outpost opened in the same location. The name is a tribute to Disney's Golden Oak Ranch in California, an 800-acre movie ranch where Disney filmed many live-action television shows and films.

Liberty Square

Liberty Square is a land unique to Walt Disney World. It exists in no other Disney theme park worldwide and was inspired by plans that Walt Disney himself had for an expansion of Disneyland.

Walt had a huge fascination with the history surrounding the creation of the United States. As early as 1957, Walt Disney had plans for a Liberty Street at Disneyland that would run parallel to Main Street and end in a cul de sac.

Cobblestones would pave the way down Liberty Street and into Liberty Square, which would be a celebration of Revolutionary War America. All the shops and exhibits would represent the types of enterprises that might be found in colonial times.

One of the major attractions in this land would be "One Nation Under God", a 27-minute show. Surrounded by a Circarama screen projecting paintings of significant episodes in U.S. history up to a Civil War climax, the audience would hear off-screen narration of the trials, decisions, and formation of the United States, including excerpts from presidential speeches.

At the conclusion, figures of all the nation's presidents (of which there were 34 in 1957, when planning started) accompanied by limited electro-mechanical movement and dramatic lighting would be seen on the enormous stage against a rear-projected image of the U.S. Capitol, as clouds panned across the sky forming an American flag and a rousing musical finale closed the show.

James Algar, who wrote the original script for the attraction as well as for Great Moments with Mr. Lincoln, remembered:

> The show was on and off at various times in the studio, but when it came time to really firm it up for Florida, when I dug out the original script, it dated back to 1961. And the Hall of Presidents was very much Walt's baby. He had this great desire to present to an audience all of the presidents of the United States on stage at once. He read into

that single idea a feeling that it would have great impact and great audience interest and fascination, and, in truth, it does.

The Hall of Presidents features all the presidents from George Washington to Barack Obama, each of them sculpted (except for Obama) by Disney Imagineer Blaine Gibson from photos and paintings.

Great attention to detail was taken even in the wardrobe to match the material used during those time periods. If a guest were to lift the pant legs of Franklin Roosevelt, they would see he was wearing polio braces just like he wore in real life.

The facade of the original Hall of Presidents in 1971 was flat brick with three windows directly above three doors into the waiting area. It wasn't until 1973 that the white veranda and breezeway were added. The date of 1787 on the front of the building refers to the year the Constitution was signed, since the focus of the original show was the Constitution and the American presidency.

With the creation of Walt Disney World, the Imagineers decided to make Walt's dream become a reality and use the new land as a preface to the story of Frontierland that recounted the expansion of America.

The decision to build this new land was also reinforced by the fact that America's bicentennial was just a few years away. When Walt Disney World opened in 1971, Liberty Square proved to be the most popular area of the new Magic Kingdom.

One of the most remarkable things about Liberty Square is that it is probably the one land at the Magic Kingdom that has had the fewest significant changes over the last 40 years. Other than some cosmetic changes like moving the flags from the bridge to surrounding the Liberty Bell, a guest visiting Liberty Square today would experience much the same as a guest in 1971.

The Liberty Bell

One of the most iconic representations of the early history of the United States originally rang from a steeple in the Pennsylvania State House (now known as Independence Hall).

The Liberty Bell was commissioned from the London firm of Lester and Pack (Whitechapel Foundry) in 1751 and displayed the phrase "Proclaim Liberty throughout all the land unto all the inhabitants thereof". The phrase was from the Book of Leviticus (25:10) in the Bible.

No one recorded when or why the Liberty Bell first cracked, but the most likely explanation is that a narrow split developed in the early 1840s after nearly 90 years of hard use. Attempts to repair the crack made it worse. Its purpose was to summon lawmakers to legislative sessions and to alert citizens to public meetings and special announcements.

The city of Philadelphia turned over the custody of the bell to the National Park Service in 1948. It was moved to a nearby glass pavilion on Independence Mall in 1976 and then to the larger Liberty Bell Center in 2003.

One of the things that changed over the years at the Magic Kingdom was the entrance to Liberty Square from the hub area of the park. In 1971, the Court of Flags representing the original 13 states led guests to the old Concord Bridge, where the colonial forces faced off with the British in 1775.

In 1991, those flags were relocated to surround the Liberty Bell that had been installed in 1989. The entrance to the land was rebuilt with the brick walls, plaque, and guardhouse that are familiar today. Stanchions now fill the holes where the flagpoles once stood.

The bridge led to a public square that would still seem somewhat similar to guests visiting the park today. The double-stacked *Admiral Joe Fowler* riverboat leisurely plied the Rivers of America starting on

October 2, 1971. It would be joined by the single stack *Richard Irvine* riverboat in 1973 that is now called the *Liberty Belle*. Irvine was the WED Imagineer in charge of the attractions, while Fowler was in charge of supervising construction inside the park.

During the bicentennial celebration of the U.S. Constitution at Walt Disney World in 1987, one of the temporary displays in Liberty Square was an authentic reproduction of the original Liberty Bell loaned from the Mount Vernon Memorial Park and Mortuary of Fair Oaks, California, through June of 1989.

However, Disney guests loved seeing the reproduction and taking photos with it, so to provide a permanent display, Disney Show Properties and Interiors purchased a new replica. It was cast by Paccard Fonderie of Annecy, France, using the original Liberty Bell mold. The new bell took its place of honor just before July 4, 1989, where it remains to this day.

The bell was made primarily of copper but also contains tin, lead, zinc, arsenic, gold, and silver. It stands eight-feet high, including stock, and weighs two-and-a-half tons. The word "Pensylvania" was an accepted alternative spelling for "Pennsylvania" and appears on the original bell. Alexander Hamilton also used that spelling in 1787 on the signature page of the United States Constitution.

Ye Olde Christmas Shoppe

When the Magic Kingdom opened in 1971, there was no Ye Olde Christmas Shoppe across the street from the Hall of Presidents.

That colonial-inspired building was devoted to three other businesses:

- Mademoiselle Lafayette's Parfumerie was one of only four perfume shops in the United States at the time that allowed customers to blend fragrances of their choice from dozens of bottles. The guest's blend could be recorded at the store for refills.
- The Silversmith Shop featured silver trinkets for purchase. Supposedly, it was the establishment of Johnny Tremain, the hero of the Esther Forbes' book that was used as the basis for the Disney live-action movie of the same name.
- Old World Antiques had authentic antiques, as well as reproductions ranging in price from five to fifteen thousand dollars.

As tastes and business needs changed, the building was converted and reopened February 5, 1996, as Ye Olde Christmas Shoppe.

Former Imagineering Show Writer M. Shawn Slater came up with the story concept for the new shop:

> Here in Liberty Square, at the close of the 18th century, Americans herald the birth of a new nation and their newfound freedoms, including the religious freedom to celebrate the traditions of Christmas. It's a simpler observance, prior to the advent of tinsel or trees or Santa Claus. Beautiful greens, adorned with fruit and pinecones and other natural items, decorate doors, sashes and mantles. Candles gleam in every window, and you can almost smell the mince pies baking.

> Ye Olde Christmas Shoppe is actually a series of buildings, storefronts with second-story residences brimming with busy craftspeople preparing for the upcoming festivities. Each shop has its own purpose and, thereby, its own character.

More formal in nature, the Music Teacher's Shop is set with recorders, mandolins and fiddles, perhaps readied for playing a ball in honor of Twelfth Night (January 6). The music on the sheets and meeting the ear is that of Watts' beloved "Joy to the World" and traditional English favorites "The Holly and the Ivy" and "I Saw Three Ships".

Next door is a Woodcarver's Shop, casual and more rough-hewn. The tools of the trade sit amidst curled shavings of pine and cherry. In the corner is a lovingly crafted hobbyhorse, and decorative holiday ornaments are all around.

Nearest the Liberty Tree is the quaint home of a family of Pennsylvania Germans, folk artists and craftsmen whose hospitality is evident in the beautiful items they offer for sale and in the pot of hot cider they keep on the stove. They are always ready to welcome townsfolk and travelers alike, spreading wishes of good cheer.

At Ye Olde Christmas Shoppe of Liberty Square, Christmas comes anew with the dawning of each day, its spirit alive forever in the hearts and homes of its residents.

The new shops were actually cleverer than this simple description suggests. Outside the music shop was a sign stating "Music & Voice Lessons by appointment Ichabod Crane, Instructor". That reference was to the protagonist in Washington Irving's famous "Legend of Sleepy Hollow" tale that has other references scattered throughout Liberty Square.

The woodcarver's shop was subtly meant to suggest Gepetto and a wooden Pinocchio figure was on a top shelf.

Outside of the Pennsylvania German household was a hand-made heart sign stating "Kepple est. 1779" to honor Walt Disney's great-great-grandfather Kepple Disney born in Ireland in 1776 which, of course, is a reference to the Revolutionary War. A tribute to Walt's grandfather, also named Kepple, is at the General Store in Frontierland on some bags of "Uncle Kepple & Sons" livestock feed.

Over the last two decades, things that helped tell the stories have been removed and rearranged, but many of the original references still exist for sharp-eyed guests.

The WDW Dapper Dans

"Dapper Dan" was a turn-of-the-last-century phrase referring to a well-dressed and groomed gentleman who was "dapper" or stylish.

In 1957, Disneyland entertainment director Tommy Walker arranged for a barbershop quartet to perform on Main Street. Disneyland's talent booker, Chuck Corson, decided to create not just a singing group on Main Street, USA, but one that could do some vaudevillian-style comedy interacting with the guests and maybe a little tap dancing.

The bass singer, T.J. Marker, who was also the leader, came up with the Dapper Dan name for the re-imagined group in 1959.

Both Walt and Lillian Disney were huge fans. Walt considered the Dapper Dans as the ambassadors of Main Street since they talked with the guests and sometimes involved them directly in the performance.

They were only given a three-month contract, something not unusual with entertainment contracts at Disney where an entertainer was never fired but just didn't have their contract renewed upon its expiration because of "ever changing entertainment needs in the park". Amusingly, many entertainers kept getting their three-month contracts renewed over and over again for decades as if it was a permanent job.

The Dapper Dans home base at WDW was the Harmony Barbershop, named after the harmony in their songs, and they sometimes serenaded guests getting a haircut. A caricature of the original group drawn by Thomas, an accomplished cartoonist, hangs in the shop.

It was Thomas who, while performing as a Dapper Dan at Disneyland, had introduced the iconic Deagan Organ Chimes into the act. Comedienne Billie Bird, a friend and vaudeville performer, had taught Thomas to play the chimes and it was her chimes that the group first used.

Each of the eight (shaker) chimes has three octaves of a single note, comprising a C scale. The organ chimes were made by the J.C. Deagan Company in Chicago, Illinois, around 1901, the year of Walt Disney's birth.

For the official dedication of Walt Disney World on October 25, 1971, the Dapper Dans sang "Lida Rose" from the popular musical *Music Man* for composer Meredith Wilson who was backstage waiting to direct the marching band that was to come down Main Street.

The Dapper Dans were actually chastised by the event managers because their harmony could be heard on stage. It didn't stop them from singing a song or two with Wilson backstage, including one of his favorite songs, "Dear Old Girl".

The original WDW Dapper Dans in 1971 were Dick Kneeland (lead), "Bub" Thomas (bass), who came from Disneyland and performed as a "Dan" for more than two decades, Jerry Siggins (baritone), and Bob Mathis (tenor).

While the group performs as a quartet, there are actually at least twelve singers assigned to the role, plus occasional substitutes. Membership has changed over the decades as various singers have left or passed away and new ones have been brought in to replace them. It has been estimated that the WDW group has sung "Goodbye, My Coney Island Baby" well over 50,000 times since the park first opened.

There are several differences between the Disneyland group and the Walt Disney World group. At Disneyland, there are some different seasonal costumes (such as for Halloween), the group is generally younger, and they use microphones to be heard above the noise of Main Street, USA

On October 13, 2014, passengers on Southwest Airlines flight #887 from Dallas to Orlando that celebrated the opening of a new non-stop air route between the Dallas Love Field airport to Orlando International Airport got a musical surprise. The WDW Dapper Dans sang tunes like "Let It Go" and "A Dream Is a Wish Your Heart Makes" to the passengers aboard the inaugural flight.

The Dapper Dans remain a beloved Disney theme park tradition that brings a greater sense of authenticity to Main Street, USA

Cinderella's Coach

The original elaborately decorated golden coach from the new Disney live-action film *Cinderella* (2015) was on display from February 1 to April 11, 2015, on the Streets of America at Disney's Hollywood Studios as a photo opportunity. Outfitted in gold leaf, it was 10-feet tall and 17-feet long.

Of course, Walt Disney World already had two Cinderella coaches that have been used for many years. There is a large, heavier one decorated with lights. There is also a smaller lightweight coach with more glass that is used for weddings and is pulled by four white ponies: currently Lady, Lacey, Lucy, and Beauty.

That smaller coach was built in Burbank, California, in 1980. It premiered at Walt Disney World in 1981 as part of the Tencennial parade and was later used in Easter and Christmas parades with a lovely Cinderella character performer smiling and waving to the crowds.

The coach has some usually unseen details such as the image of a glass slipper embedded into the glass. It later became the coach for Disney's Fairy Tale Weddings and can seat two people. Generally, it is accompanied by a driver and two footmen in sparkling white regalia.

In 1995, the larger coach was produced by Bennington Carriages who usually provided carriages for British royalty. It has cerulean blue cushions and also contains clever little details like a sculpture of two birds atop the carriage and little Suzy the mouse from the classic animated feature film *Cinderella* hitching a ride along the back.

The vines that twine along the top and sides of the coach have leaves embossed with gold. Of course, one of the distinctive differences from the smaller coach is that it can illuminate at night and seat up to four people. The coach is pulled by six full-sized white horses and is usually accompanied by three coachmen.

The Walt Disney World horses are bought on "approval" from the north when they are between three and seven years old. In general, the horses are roughly 18-hands high (or approximately 72-inches tall, since a hand is approximately 4 inches), although there are some exceptions.

For the first thirty days, the new horses are touched, brushed, and fed, but not given any work to do and are not ridden. The whole process is to get them used to the environment and allowing them to adjust to the sounds of fireworks every night from the Magic Kingdom and the constant activity of people.

Next, they are teamed with a more experienced "buddy" for wagon rides at Fort Wilderness Resort and Campground. Then, they usually graduate to do a carriage solo. This helps them get familiar with a trailer taking them to a different location, like Disney's Port Orleans Resort. In that particular location, there are fewer people and tighter paths, so it is good training.

Then, if they are considered ready, they are brought by trailer (their safe space) to backstage at the Magic Kindgom to hear the sounds of the parade and get used to the costumed characters.

Sometimes, they are incorporated into the parade before getting the role of pulling the trolley or Cinderella's coach.

There were two ponies that were born at the Tri-Circle D Ranch many years ago (Levi and Blaze), but they are considered "oops" babies. Disney was unaware the mares were pregnant when they were purchased. That is not an oversight that happens today. There are no additional "oops" babies because all the male horses are geldings. That aspect not only prevents breeding but also "mellows out" the horses to interact with guests.

Mexico's The Three Caballeros

The Mexico Pavilion opened in October 1982 featuring a boat ride attraction entitled El Rio del Tiempo (The River of Time) that took visitors on a leisurely cruise through the history of Mexico, from Mayan high priests to modern merchants.

In 2007, a new storyline was introduced where guests would still enjoy a boat tour (now called the Gran Fiesta Tour) experiencing the arts, culture, and history of Mexico, but with addition of the famous Three Caballeros: Donald Duck (representing the United States), the parrot Jose Carioca (Brazil, and representing all of South America), and the rooster Panchito Pistoles (Mexico). The trio appeared in Disney's feature compilation film *The Three Caballeros* (1944). In the film, after singing their memorable theme song, they all go on a magic serape ride over Mexico, in a mix of animation and live action.

However, the new version of the boat tour hits a snag when Panchito and Jose Carioca discover their amigo, Donald Duck, has gone sightseeing in Mexico on the very day the famous Three Caballeros are to perform a reunion concert in Mexico City.

In charge of this new revision reuniting the Three Cabelleros was director George Scribner (who was also the director of Mickey's PhilharMagic in Fantasyland) and animation director Eric Goldberg (supervising animator on *Aladdin*'s genie and co-director on *Pocahontas*).

The new film elements combined traditional character animation overlaid onto film clips of live background footage that were projected onto a series of screens framed by dimensional walls, arches, and rockwork to set the scenes. Props, set facades, lighting, and the sound system also were refurbished and enhanced.

When this version of the Gran Fiesta Tour opened on April 6, 2007, the final scene featured a large screen with animation of the Three Caballeros performing together. On December 4, 2015, this finale was replaced with audio-animatronics figures of the three title characters who had first appeared at WDW over forty-five years earlier.

Those figures originally were part of the Mickey Mouse Revue, an attraction that opened at the Magic Kingdom on October 1, 1971, and featured multiple small audio-animatronics figures of popular Disney cartoon characters designed and animated by Imagineer Bill Justice.

Over the years, the popularity of the Mickey Mouse Revue waned. It was closed at Magic Kingdom on September 14, 1980, and was shipped to Tokyo Disneyland where it opened on April 15, 1983. It continued to operate there for twenty-six years until it was replaced by Mickey's PhilharMagic in 2009.

At that time, Epcot management made arrangements to save, purchase, and have shipped to the United States the Three Caballeros figures from the attraction.

Unfortunately, due to a misunderstanding, there was no money left in the budget to install them in the new Gran Fiesta Tour attraction as originally intended. So for many years, they were stored safely backstage at Epcot as each year's budget kept getting directed to other needs in the park.

The figures made their next public appearance at Disney's Contemporary Resort as part of D23's Destination D: Walt Disney World 40th in May 2011, when the Walt Disney Archives curated a special exhibit honoring four decades of the theme park and needed items that didn't incur any costs from being shipped from the West Coast.

Eric Goldberg recalled:

> We always thought the Three Caballeros would be perfect for the Mexico Pavilion. And it's a great way to introduce the Disney characters to the Epcot pavilions and keep them within the context of the travel and tourism story of the World Showcase.

The Norway Pavilion

The Norway Pavilion was the eleventh and final (so far) country added to Epcot's World Showcase. The official dedication of the Norway Pavilion was on Friday June 3, 1988.

As early as 1979, the Disney company was in discussions with the country of Denmark for a pavilion at World Showcase. As late as 1983, Disney was still in discussions with LEGO to help fund that particular pavilion.

Still hoping that the negotiations would prove successful, Disney built the outdoors bathrooms for the Denmark Pavilion to be available at the October 1982 opening and they continue to operate today.

It was the Norwegian company Selmer-Sande and Kloster that first started the work of a Scandinavian pavilion celebrating Nordic culture in Epcot.

In 1983, it was determined that the pavilion would be devoted not just to Denmark but also Sweden and Norway, and would open in 1987. However, only Norway raised the necessary funding, through Norwegian Showcase (NorShow), a consortium of eleven companies established to pay for the pavilion and represent Norwegian interests.

NorShow president Gunnar Jerman said his organization contributed $34 million for the final pavilion. The figure included a $2 million contribution from the Norwegian government and an $8 million government loan to NorShow.

NorShow put up over two-thirds of the construction cost for the pavilion with Disney picking up the tab for the rest.

The company battled cost overruns because WDI designed and built the entire pavilion, even though Scandinavian architects were involved as well, and in doing so overhead costs became inflated. The final cost of the pavilion was estimated at close to $46 million.

Norway did not pay Disney the extra costs to hook it up to the electrical grid for the night-time fireworks extravaganza so the pavilion would light up. Norway assumed that the spilled light from the Mexico and China pavilions would illuminate the pavilion adequately without incurring additional expenses to use an already antiquated system. Disney refused to pick up the added expense either, assuming that NorShow would eventually acquiesce, until it was too late.

NorShow shared the profit from sales of food and souvenirs in the pavilion. The first $3.2 million in profit went to NorShow, and the next $400,000 to Disney. After that, NorShow kept 60 percent of all profit and Disney received 40 percent.

The Norway Pavilion was designed to look like a Norwegian village, including a detailed Stave church based on one from 1212 A.D. that was preserved in the Norwegian Folk Museum in Oslo. In the 12th and 13th centuries more than 800 stave churches were built, eventually reaching a peak of over 1,300.

Unfortunately, most were destroyed for a variety of reasons or fell apart from neglect because the wood couldn't continually withstand the harsh Norwegian weather. Today, only about two dozen Stave churches remain.

Four styles of Norwegian architecture were showcased to represent the different areas of the country: Setesdal, Bergen, Oslo, and Ålesund.

The architecture of the Gallery and the Puffin's Roost show the inland farm log-construction of Setesdal. The Fjording shop with its gabled windows captures the spirit of Bergen. Restaurant Akershus represents Oslo, with the exterior resembling its namesake fortress in that city. Alesund is typified by the white stucco and stone trimmed Informasjon and Maelstrom buildings.

During the first year that the pavilion was open, there were on average 150 requests per week from guests interested in traveling to Norway. On source claimed that during the first year of the pavilion's operation, tourism to Norway increased by 500–700% from the previous year.

Norway's Maelstrom and Frozen Ever After

The official dedication of the Norway Pavilion was on Friday June 3, 1988, but because of glitches in the attraction (including drenching passengers in the North Sea scene), Maelstrom did not open until about a month later, on July 5.

An Epcot press release at the time described the attraction:

> Visitors take a fantasy voyage that departs a modern-day village on a Norwegian fjord and journeys up a cascading waterway into the Norway of old. The trip is aboard small ships patterned after the dragon-headed craft of Eric the Red and his fellow explorers.

The boats were some of the first concept art work done by Imagineer Joe Rohde for Walt Disney World. It was also some of the last work done by famed Imagineer Jack Ferges, who built the model for the ride vehicle ship which was replicated in fiberglass for use in the attraction.

Originally, Maelstrom was to be called SeaVenture and the concept was more mythological in tone. Guests would be riding along a 946-foot water flume encountering trolls and gnomes and the legends about them. Another proposal was Vikings on their way to the Rainbow Bridge in Vallhalla.

The Norwegian sponsors (NorShow) disliked the concept and wanted the attraction to be more of a travelogue to encourage increased tourism. NorShow gave the Imagineers a list of items they wanted shown in the attraction that they felt uniquely related to the story of Norway, including Vikings, a fishing village, an eleven-foot-tall polar bear, a fjord, an oil rig, and perhaps, if there was room, a troll or two.

Attraction Designer Bob Kurzweil came up with the new approach that it would be a time travel experience through the history of Norway beginning with the earliest folklore and ending in modern-day Norway to incorporate everything that the sponsors wanted.

In the first full year of operation, over 5.7 million guests rode the popular Maelstrom attraction.

NorShow sold back its interest in the Norway Pavilion to Disney in 1992, but the Norwegian government continued to support the pavilion with a contribution of $200,000 a year for the next ten years, before dropping all financial support in 2002.

Becoming the sole support of the pavilion, the Disney company looked for a way to increase revenue and attendance. The unexpected success of the movie *Frozen* (2013) spurred the idea of an animation overlay similar to the ones done for the Mexico and Living Seas attractions.

In Frozen Ever After, Queen Elsa, Princess Anna, Kristoff, Olaf, trolls, and Marshmallow (the giant snowman) join guests on their boat journey on a "summer snow day" through the frozen willow forest, past Troll Valley, and up to the North Mountain to Elsa's ice palace. The attraction ends in the Bay of Arendelle.

Along the way, state-of-the-art audio-animatronics, such as Sven the reindeer, are in the new scenes as well as elements from the animated short *Frozen Fever* (2015) including the Snowgies, the mini-snow creatures created from Elsa's sneezes.

Composers Bobby Lopez and Kristen Anderson-Lopez created new lyrics to the original *Frozen* (2013) film songs they wrote, and all of the original voice talent from the film returned and recorded new dialogue and songs for the attraction.

Imagineer Wyatt Winter, who worked on the attraction, said:

> The original animated film was heavily influenced by Norwegian culture and the filmmakers conducted extensive research in Norway. Our team began our process in the same manner, visiting places in Norway that heavily influenced our work. While there's clearly a *Frozen* twist to our story, honoring the culture and traditions of Norway was always among our guiding principles.

The Rose and Crown Pub

In the United Kingdom, "Rose and Crown" is the twelfth most popular name for a pub, sharing it with over four hundred other pubs. The origin of the rose and crown images goes back several centuries.

King Edward III used a golden rose as a personal badge, and two of his sons adapted it by changing the color: John of Gaunt, 1st Duke of Lancaster, used a red rose, and Edmund of Langley, 1st Duke of York, used a white rose.

The dynastic conflicts between their descendants are collectively called the Wars of the Roses. In 1485 Henry Tudor, a descendant of Lancaster, defeated Richard III of the York dynasty and married Richard's niece Elizabeth of York. Since then the combined red-and-white Tudor rose, often crowned, has been a symbol of the monarchy of England and demonstrates loyalty to the monarchy.

So, when Disney decided to create an authentic "public house" in the U.K. pavilion at Epcot, they selected that name but created their own distinct design of the two images that was reminiscent of the signs that Imagineers had seen in numerous historic pubs throughout Great Britain.

After deciding on the number of signs required, refining the rough design, and negotiating the projected budget, Bass Ale and Stout, the pub's sponsor, gave its approval.

Color comps were produced and a rough working drawing was developed. Finally, after all the costs were computed, Imagineering decided to offer the job of creating the finished sign to a freelance illustrator. Bruce McCurdy of WED Graphics said:

> Originally, we were going to go outside, but the Studio Sign Shop in Burbank showed an interest and when we saw Charles Opie's original rendition, we loved it and went with his design.

Underneath the image is the Latin motto Otium Cum Dignitate, meaning Leisure with Dignity.

Disney based their version of a typical pub on four different styles of British pubs, according to the publicity release when Epcot Center opened.

The city or "street" pub dating back from the 1890s Victorian city center features brick-and-wood paneling on the facade and relates to the interior mahogany bar and the etched glass and molded plaster ceiling. It constitutes the main entrance area.

The Dickensian pub inspired by the Cheshire Cheese pub in London offers a brick-walled flagstone terrace with covered tables, slate roof, and half-timbered Elizabethan styled exterior.

The waterfront or "river" pub, facing the World Showcase Lagoon, is represented by a facade with a modest stone building, clay tiled roof, decorative doorways, and a stone terrace with an iron fence lining the village inn-styled dining room. (Nearby in the lagoon is a replica of the 137-mile-long Grand Union Canal. The replica once had two locks, one at each end, which have since been removed.)

The country pub from the suburbs of the 17th and 18th centuries is represented by a slate roof and plaster exterior with stone quoined corners.

Authentic pints of British ales, lagers, and stouts that are available, including Bass, Harp, Guinness, Boddingtons, and Strongbow. The menu offers traditional British specialties such as Harry Ramsden's Fish and Chips and Bangers & Mash (sausage and mashed potatoes).

Guests were so anxious to get just the fish and chips that Disney eventually offered a separate cart for that menu item alone and then built the quick service Yorkshire County Fish Shop outside the area, resembling the country pub.

Japan's Candy Wizards

In the days of the Qin Dynasty, nearly 2,400 years ago, the son of a poor Chinese scholar fell in love with a wealthy nobleman's daughter.

His heart ached for the lovely maid but his head told him he could never marry without money to support an aristocratic bride. Remembering an old pastime his mother practiced, the young man began to toy with bits of rice-flour dough.

With his thoughts focused on his beloved, his hands fashioned ornate sculpture from the dough. Horses, unicorns, and fanciful beasts sprang from the mixture.

Soon the youth was attracting crowds of onlookers fascinated by the beautiful wonders he created. In time, the young artist was able to earn his fortune and eventually the hand of the girl he loved.

This is the legend of Amezaiku, a candy-art sculpture craft passed orally from generation to generation through China and Japan. Currently, there are only fifteen people officially trained in the art which is reminiscent of glass blowing.

Amezaiku, which translates as "sweet candy craft", is only one of many endangered traditions. It is also sometimes referred to as zinen houni, or "dream fantasy".

A rice starch syrup is boiled until it becomes dough-like, malleable, and transparent, like taffy. It is heated to roughly two hundred degrees over charcoal to make it pliable, then divided into small portions and kneaded and pulled into small balls. During this process, it takes on a pure-white color and often the artist would add a food color like pink, blue, or green. The ball is placed on the end of small chopstick.

The artist must then work quickly to form the animal figures at the tip of a chopstick, using tiny candy scissors, tweezers, and his fingers. The artist would also use a hand fan to occasionally cool and harden portions. Further decoration and detail is painted on the candy creature with edible dye food colorings.

Animals and insects are common shapes created by Amezaiku to delight younger children.

The Japan Pavilion in World Showcase was home to two of the top Amezaiku artists working in the United States.

Masaji Terasawa, a native of Osaka, began working at Epcot in the 1980s. He began as a street performer in Japan and then moved to the Los Angeles area in the early 1970s. At Epcot, he would sometimes perform blindfolded or dance to taped music in slow rhythmic movements similar to traditional Tai Ji Quan.

He is considered a master of the art and trained Shinobu "Shan" Ichiyanagi for three years as his apprentice. Terasawa remains a much in-demand performer at schools, festivals, private parties, and other events. He said: "I like to show traditional Japanese art with humor and audience participation."

Miyuki Sugimori first appeared at the pavilion in 1996 and continued working until her final show on November 23, 2013. From Tokyo, Miyuki learned the craft starting in 1989 from her grandfather, Mr. Kinura, who was a renowned candy artist.

She remains the first and only woman to receive training in Amezaiku in Japan. She has a daughter, Shido, and when asked by a guest if she plans on teaching her daughter this gift, she replied, "No, she cries because her hands hurt!" (from the temperature).

The "stage" for these candy wizards was a simple cart located outside the front entrance of the Mitsukoshi department store. The cart was equipped with heating elements to keep the candy pliable and also had fans to cool down the finished hot pieces and set the design before it would be handed to guests who had gathered around to watch the performance.

While the artists often sculpted frogs, swans, alligators, tigers, elephants, and other animals, many guests requested winged dragons and unicorns. The candy was edible, but guests often tried to preserve the art in a clear plastic bag kept away from heat.

Japan's Goju-No-To Pagoda

The eighty-three-foot tall blue-roofed Goju-no-to Pagoda at the entrance to the Japan Pavilion is fashioned after the pagoda at Horyuji Temple in Nara which was built in the 8th century as a center of art, architecture, and scholarship. That original building is acknowledged as one of the oldest wooden buildings still standing in the world.

Japanese pagodas are less elaborate and brightly colored than the ones in China that inspired them. Two factors are involved with this difference. First, the Japanese love for purity of form and their quest for simplicity. Second, Japan suffers ten percent of all earthquakes on the planet, including some of the most intense; simpler construction alleviates damage and the need to rebuild.

The original design by the Imagineers was much too fancy since it incorporated elements from a variety of different pagodas. The Japan Pavilion sponsors asked them to tone it down signficantly because it looked too much like a Chinese pagoda with its bright colors and ornamentation.

So the Imagineers used the Horyuji Temple, known as the Temple of the Flourishing Law, built in 607 A.D. that stood 122-feet tall as inspiration. In December 1993, Horyuji, because of its many connections to Buddhist heritage, became the first treasure of any kind in Japan to be selected by UNESCO as part of the World Heritage Sites, cultural and natural sites that show "outstanding universal value".

The plaque in front of the Epcot pagoda reads:

> The Goju-No-To, or Five Story Pagoda, traditionally represents the five elements from which Buddhists believe all things in the universe are produced. In ascending order, the elements are earth, water, fire, wind and sky. Similar in design to the Horyuji Temple in Nara, this Gojo-No-To stands nearly 83-feet tall. It is a true monument to the skills and accomplishments of early Japanese architects.

The bells on the corners and in the spire are there to scare away bad spirits when the wind blows. When the pavilion first opened, the constant sound of the bells was distracting to guests, so the Imagineers tamped them down to ring less frequently and loudly. The curved edges of the roofs are meant to impale bad spirits if they seek to enter the building.

Above the pagoda is a bronze, nine-ringed sorin, or spire, with gold wind chimes and a water flame. The rings are called kurin and the bells on them futaku. Of course, its height also helps it serve a very important function as a lightning rod since central Florida is the lightning strike capital of the world.

Matsuriza, a group of synchronized Japanese taiko drummers, perform five days a week at the base of the pagoda.

Taiko means "fat drum" in Japanese. Traditional Japanese drumming has been performed for centuries (which explains why the group is located at the lower balcony of the pagoda) during religious ceremonies, harvest festivals, and even during battles to encourage soldiers and scare the enemy.

The drums can range in size from six inches to six feet in diameter, and so require great strength and stamina.

Takemasa Ishikura began performing as a drummer at the Epcot pavilion in 1983 under the leadership of Yoshihisa Ishikura, who returned to Japan in 1998. Takemasa took over, creating the group known as the Matsuriza Japanese Traditional Taiko Drummers. According to a Disney publicity release:

> Founded by Takoma's Ishikura in 1998, this percussion troupe is part of the relatively recent art-form of ensemble taiko drumming that is sweeping around the world. Matsuriza performs both traditional arrangements and its own compositions at locales around the world.

O Canada!

There were three fiberglass totem poles in the pavilion since its opening in 1982, but they were merely decorative and intended like the Trading Post to broadly represent the Indian tribes of the Northwest.

The Northwest Mercantile was meant to represent the French and English frontiersmen, trappers, prospectors, loggers, and traders who inhabited the area during the earliest years of the country. The outside of the building is decorated with authentic tools and snowshoes that were found by the Imagineers during their explorations of Canada.

The Maritime Provinces of Prince Edward Island, Nova Scotia and New Brunswick are represented by the stone work on the level with shops above the Trading Post. On the left hand side, the architecture references the British influence (and was intended to house the never-installed Canadian Tourism Center offices) and on the right hand side, the French influence.

The Hotel du Canada is patterned after the Chateau Laurier in Ottawa and the Hotel du Frontenac in Quebec. This French gothic design is reminiscent of the hotels that were built during the expansion of the Canadian railroad system.

The hotel building may look six- to seven-stories tall but is only three stories tall due to the use of forced perspective, with the bricks and windows (appropriately decorated with scaled-down items) growing progressively smaller as the building rises.

Just beyond the hotel is some of the last work done by Imagineer Fred Joerger to re-create a sense of the Canadian Rockies. Imagineers flew over the Canadian mountains and took pictures to develop a topographical map. They then created a Styrofoam model and used a computer to draw a three-dimensional picture showing horizontal and vertical features as well as depth.

An enlarged version was adapted and used as the master blueprint for the steel structure which was then covered with Gunite, the same cement used in swimming pool construction. Joerger and his crew then textured it all by hand, including the thirty foot tall waterfall.

The challenge was having live trees in an artificial environment which was solved by using a containerized plant system where trees were planted in five-foot-deep planters with built-in irrigation and drainage systems. This also proved useful when the trees started to grow too large for the appropriate forced perspective and could be easily replaced.

In 1998, the Disney company employed Tsimshian artist David Boxley from Alaska, noted for his decades-long creation of totem poles, to carve an authentic 30-foot totem pole to replace the one near the Trading Post.

During the carving process, the seven-hundred-pound red cedar log was laid on its side on a raised platform in front of the pavilion. Boxley laboriously worked on it and interacted with guests until it was erected next to the Trading Post in April 1998.

This beautiful totem pole tells the tale from the Pacific Northwest Indians of Raven and Sky Chief. When the trickster Raven came to earth, the people lived in the dark without shadows and without the sun, moon, or stars. Raven begins a search for light. He notices Sky Chief keeps a bright light in his home hidden away in a box, and so transforms himself into Sky Chief's grandson. When Sky Chief brings out the box to show his "grandson" the golden ball of light, Raven grabs the shiny ball, turns back into his true form, and flies up into the sky where he tosses the light so all people can enjoy the sun, the moon, and the stars.

Boxley intentionally placed two small green Hidden Mickeys under each of the bending elbows near the top of the pole.

Mission: SPACE

The Flight to the Moon attraction that mirrored the one at Disneyland didn't open in Walt Disney World's Tomorrowland until December 24, 1971.

It was replaced by Mission to Mars on March 21, 1975 (since Americans had actually walked on the moon in 1969), although it retained a similar show format. The attraction remained until October 1993 when it was superseded by ExtraTERRORestrial Alien Encounter.

These earlier attractions were meant to give theme park guests a small glimpse of outer space exploration, but the technology did not exist at the time for it to be a more accurate experience. Mission to Mars had guests enter a circular auditorium with screens both above and below so they could watch their flight in progress. References from that vintage space attraction are included in WDW's Tomorrowland.

In the spirit of that attraction, Mission: SPACE opened at Epcot in 2003. It was influenced by a science-fiction film directed by Brian DePalma entitled Mission to Mars (2000) and starring actor Gary Sinise who appears as the CapCom narrator in the attraction.

The movie was made by Touchstone Pictures and distributed by Buena Vista Pictures, both Disney divisions. Despite its elaborate special effects and strong cast, it garnered neither financial or critical success but elements from the film were already incorporated into the attraction.

It was part of a Disney initiative to have the themes of Disney park attractions like the original Tomorrowland Mission to Mars converted into feature films that eventually resulted in the much more successful Pirates of the Caribbean film series.

The storyline for Mission: SPACE is that it is the year 2036 at the International Space Training Center (ISTC) and new trainees have come to see if they have "the right stuff" to be the first humans to go to Mars.

The centrifugal simulator hardware used in Mission: SPACE to create a sense of g-force during the mission was designed and built by Environmental Tectonics Corporation of Pennsylvania. ETC later sued Disney for non-payment of the full amount agreed upon and sharing proprietary design details with competitors. Both companies settled in an out-of-court settlement in 2009.

A Disney publicity release claimed that it took more than 650 Walt Disney Imagineers more than 350,000 hours (the equivalent of 40 years of time) to develop the attraction over a five-year period.

The intense physical experience caused some guests to become ill or disoriented for a variety of reasons, with a fourteen-year-old boy dying in June 2005 after riding the attraction. In May 2006, Disney introduced the Green and Orange versions of Mission: SPACE. The Green version did not include the centrifuge pressure, while the Orange version remained the same as the original.

Several tributes to the earlier WDW space exploration attractions can be found in Mission: SPACE. The deserted mission control room at the end of the queue includes the original control boards from Mission to Mars. One of the videos on the monitors is a live-action crash landing of an albatross which elicited laughs when shown in the Mission to Mars attraction as an unidentified intrusion into the launch area.

Mr. Johnson, who was the audio-animatronics host of Mission to Mars is repeatedly paged—"Attention, Mr. Johnson, check the radar, sector M2M ("Mission 2 Mars")—while trainees are waiting to board their vehicles.

Other hidden treasures abound in the attraction, including logos from the former Horizons attraction that was in this location to a genuine NASA Lunar Roving Vehicle (LRV), suspended from the ceiling in the Sim Lab, that is one of only four in existence, and is on loan from the Smithsonian. It is the only LRV constructed by NASA that is not on the moon.

Sorcerer's Hat

The centerpiece for the 100 Years of Magic celebration was the supposedly temporary sorcerer's hat at Disney-MGM Studios, unveiled on September 28, 2001. According to Disney publicity, it represented "the magic of show business and the entertainment wizardry of Disney".

The park was originally intended to represent the Golden Age of Hollywood of the 1940s, so it was appropriate to use an image that appeared in the animated feature *Fantasia* (1940). The character of the sorcerer in the film, Yensid (Disney spelled backwards), was based on Walt Disney himself, including his famous arched eyebrow.

It was apparent that Disney-MGM Studios needed a clear icon to identify the park on merchandise and on marketing. The Magic Kingdom had Cinderella Castle. Epcot had Spaceship Earth. Disney's Animal Kingdom had the Tree of Life.

The Chinese theater became the default icon for many guests who assumed it was the doppleganger for the famous Disney castles at the end of Main Street, but the theater already had a colorful history and it was rumored that Disney had restrictions on its use.

The amount of concrete poured for the foundation of the hat would have filled a football field one-foot deep, according to Disney publicity.

Disney-MGM Studios had been open for twelve years before the placement of the "temporary" hat. The hat survived over fourteen years, so many guests assumed it was always there.

During the 100 Years of Magic celebration, there were interactive kiosks underneath the hat where guests were encouraged to learn more about the life and career of Walt Disney. After the celebration, the kiosks were removed and the area was converted into a pin-selling location since the retail division of the Disney company had shouldered the cost for building it in the first place.

Here are the official figures for the composite fiberglass hat when it was originally constructed. It took roughly nine months to build.

- Hat Height: 100 feet. Since it is resting atop the ears and canted to the side, the actual summit was 122 feet.
- Icon Weight: 156 tons.
- Hat Weight (the brim and hat only, excluding the ears and support structure): 27 tons.
- Hat Size (as wardrobe): 605 and 7/8.
- Mickey, wearing this hat, would be 350 feet tall, based off of scaling the real-life costumed characters in the park.
- The hat is painted with a custom paint technique called "chameleon paint" which will cause the hat to shift in color as guests move closer and around it. Disney used enough of this automotive-type paint to cover 500 Cadillacs.
- The ears will appear to change colors, surface shapes, and sparkle with internal pixie dust lighting.
- The component of the hat include 6 stars and 2 moons, 13 total air vents, 13,493 bolts holding the hat together, and 17,000 feet (or 57 football fields) of underground utility piping.
- Hat interior space: 59,458 cubic feet.
- Mickey hand height: 39' 6".
- Mickey hand width: 32' 8¼".
- Left ear height (to top of ear): 61' 3".
- Right ear height " to top of ear): 39' 2¼".

On April 11, 2003, a new sculpture debuted, replacing the 100 Years of Magic Celebration logo under the Sorcerer Mickey icon. This permanent sculpture featured gold ribbons decorated with silver stars and was located adjacent to a merchandise venue under the icon.

The structure's removal began on January 7, 2015, and was completed 49 days later, on February 25, 2015.

The Twilight Zone Tower of Terror

The narration warns:

> One stormy night long ago, five people stepped through the door of an elevator and into a nightmare. That door is opening once again, and this time, it's opening for you.

It was Halloween night, October 31, 1939, when a freakish thunder-and-lightning storm descended on the Hollywood hills while the elite of the film community found sanctuary in the prestigious and popular Hollywood Tower Hotel's elegant lobby. Outside the hotel is a plaque indicating that the hotel was built in 1917.

Among those checking in that night were young singer Carolyn Crosson and her boyfriend Gilbert London as well as child actress Sally Shine in blonde curls and frilly dress (reminiscent of actress Shirley Temple) with her stern governess Emeline Partridge. Sally clutches a Mickey Mouse doll. Overworked bellman Dewey Todd assisted them into the elevator.

They stepped in, the doors closed, and seconds later the elevator, its passengers, and several sections of the upper stories of the hotel vanished when lightning struck the building, leaving a burnt scar and a gaping hole on the outside.

The hotel is frozen in a limbo of time and space, and while the exterior has fallen into disrepair over the years with overgrown vegetation, the interior remains frighteningly like it was that fateful 1939 Halloween night.

The directory in the lobby is an anagram that spells "evil Tower UR doomed". The mahjongg game in the lobby was set up by professional players.

What makes it spooky is that if the players left the table they would have pushed their chairs away from the table to get up. Their chairs are positioned as if people were sitting there playing the game and then just disappeared. On the wall in the lobby by the concierge's desk is a "13 Diamond" award. (In actuality the award would only go up to five. Thirteen is an unlucky number.)

The video depicting that horrific evening was directed by Joe Dante who also directed a segment of the 1983 movie version of *The Twilight Zone*. The set that they used to film those scenes for the attraction was built in Hollywood for the shooting and then dismantled and reassembled in the lobby of the actual attraction in Florida so it would look exactly as it was in the video.

Imagineers screened each of the 156 episodes of *The Twilight Zone* television series at least twice. The attraction is littered with references from the show.

Performer Mark Silverman was selected from hundreds of others to provide the voice of Rod Serling by Serling's widow, who made the final selection after listening to him on audio tape.

The design of the building was inspired by the Mission Inn in Riverside, the Biltmore Hotel in Los Angeles, and especially the exterior façade of the Chateau Marmont Hotel in Hollywood, built in 1927.

The attraction is only 199 feet tall because Federal regulations would have required a flashing red beacon to warn aircraft if it were 200 or more feet tall. It is composed of 1,500 tons of steel, 145,800 cubic feet of concrete, and 27,000 individual roof tiles.

It officially opened July 22, 1994 and quickly became the most popular attraction at the park.

The narration ends with:

> A warm welcome back to those of you who made it, and a friendly word of warning, something you won't find in any guidebook. The next time you check into a deserted hotel on the dark side of Hollywood, make sure you know just what kind of vacancy you're filling. Or you may find yourself a permanent resident...of the Twilight Zone.

The Madison Mermaid Statue

Near the restrooms next to the Studio Catering Company quick serve restaurant at Disney's Hollywood Studios is a statue that has been there since the park first opened in 1989. It is a classic demure mermaid sitting in a curved platform supported by four dolphins who are spouting water. The fountain is a prop from the film *Splash* (1984).

Splash seems an insignificant film to be enshrined at Disney's Hollywood Studios, but it was the first film made by the new Touchstone division of Disney films in 1984 that was created for movies with content not appropriate for a general Disney audience.

The film was a huge financial success. Made on a budget of eight million dollars, it grossed over six million dollars on just its opening weekend and went on to become the tenth highest grossing film of the year. Directed by Ron Howard, *Splash* recounts the story of Allen Bauer (Tom Hanks) and his encounter with a mermaid named Madison (Daryl Hannah) and how it changed his life.

The beach where Tom Hanks encounters the mermaid was filmed at Castaway Cay (then known as Gorda Cay). According to legend, Ariel in *The Little Mermaid* (1989) was originally going to be blonde, but was made a redhead to distinguish her from the blonde Madison.

The plaque states:

> SPLASH 1984. This mermaid was Madison's gift to Allen. Although it appears to be made of brass and stone, it was fabricated entirely out of fiberglass at the Walt Disney Studios Scenic Shop.

> The molds used to produce the mermaid and dolphins were originally created for ice sculptures seen in the Walt Disney Productions' film *Herbie Goes Bananas*.

Splash was a favorite film of then CEO Michael Eisner and he greenlit a sequel called *Splash Too* with an entirely new cast and produced for roughly three million dollars. It was the first film to be completely shot at the new Disney-MGM Studios and was released in 1988.

Ron Howard told Marilyn Beck of the *Chicago Tribune* on February 28, 1985:

> Because of the urgency Michael Eisner has placed on *Splash Too*, I'll limit myself to co-producing it with Brian Glazer. It will not be a copycat sequel. They'll come back to land, but there will still be plenty of underwater action.

Eisner hoped the sequel would spin off into a popular television series which is another reason for the statue to be featured so prominently at the theme park. Unfortunately, the sequel didn't have the same impact critically or financially as the original.

Besides putting the statue in the park, Eisner intended that in 1989 at Pleasure Island there would be a sunken bar nightclub called Madison's Dive filled with sailors telling tall fish tales, including one about an elusive mermaid who would occasionally swim by one of the windows below sea level.

Some of the effects such as the sinking ship in the bottle were later incorporated into the Adventurer's Club. Madison's Dive would have been built on a pier that jutted out into Lake Buena Vista between the Adventurer's Club and the XZFR Rockin' Rollerdrome.

The fountain was damaged in 2004 when Hurricane Charley broke off the mermaid, but it was repaired and remains on display.

The Creation of Muppet*Vision 3D

Former Imagineer Mark Eades worked on Muppet*Vision 3D and shared these stories with me in 2010.

Bill Prady, a Henson writer, was tasked with organizing the ideas into a story and after several meetings he and Jim Henson had the first storyline. It was essentially an introduction to Bean Bunny and all the other Muppets had cameos.

[Note: Bean Bunny first appeared in 1986 as the star of the TV special The Tale of the Bunny Picnic. In 1989, Bean joined the cast of The Jim Henson Hour.]

We all pointed out how theme park attractions based on existing characters usually worked better where there was some familiarity with their universe. Star Tours worked because it still had all those familiar Star Wars universe items in it.

We suggested that the same thing was needed for this attraction, in particular because it had a stage and a proscenium just like in the Muppet Show—as Henson became more intrigued with breaking down that fourth wall, the ideas of having characters in the theater evolved and the story evolved.

Jim Henson was very involved with the project. He was genuinely interested in doing theme park attractions. His natural curiosity and openness and receptiveness to new ideas made him a perfect fit to work with at Imagineering. It was a two-year process from concept to finished production.

The entire project was done in California, except for the actual installation. The film was shot almost entirely on Stage 3 at the Disney Studios, the same stage that 20,000 Leagues Under the Sea (1954) was filmed on. We needed the water tank for Miss Piggy's musical number.

The Miss Piggy number was the first sequence filmed. It took several days. Then we moved over to the other side of the stage for the Muppet Labs sequences, both the hallway and the Honeydew set. Then we went outside to the old Town Square from Something Wicked This Way

Comes (1983) for the brick-wall-blowing-up shot and the last shot when Kermit comes in on the fire truck ladder.

Then we moved back to the other side of stage 3 where the Miss Piggy set was which was now black for the entire patriotic finale which was done against a black backdrop.

The film had been completed way under budget, and after a test showing with everyone we knew we needed to tweak a few things. The middle of the film kind of fell flat. So the plan was that everyone would come back after a few weeks off and we would get together to figure it out.

I was on vacation as a tourist in Washington D.C. with my family when the word came that Jim had died.

We came home the next day. About a month later we got together to figure things out with the Henson creative team including Frank Oz, Bill Prady, and others. We storyboarded some new scenes, including a slightly different bit about Bean Bunny running away, and scheduled a re-shoot.

Frank Oz directed the new scenes and we did a temporary mix up at Skywalker Ranch. Another test showing and the film was signed off. Then, the Henson family asked that everyone involved from their side walk away and we had to finish the film, including all the Waldo CGI, much of which was added as a result of the new stuff, without them, including all the performers.

It was an example of the kinds of attractions Disney could and should be doing. We at Imagineering and Theme Park Productions were extremely proud of it.

The Brown Derby

There were four Brown Derby restaurants in the Los Angeles area (Hollywood, Beverly Hills, Los Feliz, and Wilshire Boulevard), but only the first one on Wilshire Boulevard was in the shape of a derby hat.

The one most frequented by Walt Disney was the restaurant on Vine Street, a half block south of Hollywood Boulevard, that opened in 1929 and was operated by his friend Bob Cobb who took over in 1934. There is a photo of a smiling Walt and his wife Lillian enjoying a Cobb salad there from 1939.

The restaurant was in the center of broadcasting studios, theaters, and movie studios, so it became a popular location for celebrities and for making deals, which is why the booths were designed so that people could be easily seen.

The architect, Carl Jules Weyl, later became a Warner Bros art director. He designed the iconic Rick's Café in the classic film *Casablanca* (1942) where Rick (Humphrey Bogart) had an apartment office above the restaurant similar to the one designed for owner Bob Cobb above the Hollywood Brown Derby.

It is this version of the famous restaurant that is re-created at Disney's Hollywood Studios from a licensing agreement in 1987. The original restaurant was closed in 1985 because of fire and earthquake damage and demolished in 1994. Part of the re-creation includes a private dining room known as the Bamboo Room where today WDW guests can dine with an Imagineer.

After midnight in 1937, Bob Cobb was awakened by the pounding on the door by his friend, theater entrepreneur Sid Grauman of Grauman's Chinese Theater. The restaurant had long been closed for the night. To help sober up his friend before sending him on his way, Cobb went into the kitchen to see what leftovers he could find.

Opening the huge refrigerator, he pulled out a head of lettuce, an avocado, some romaine, watercress, tomatoes, some cold breast of chicken, a hard-boiled egg, chives, cheese, bacon, and some old-fashioned French dressing.

He started chopping it up very fine to blend the disparate items together and give it some substance. Reportedly, Grauman had just had some dental work done and could not chew easily.

It did the trick and the next day Grauman dropped by again during operating hours and ordered a "Cobb Salad". Other patrons saw it and also ordered it and it became a sensation. Movie mogul Jack Warner often sent his personal chauffeur over to pick up a carton of the salad.

Millions of salads have been sold over the decades and it is the most popular entrée at the Disney version of the restaurant.

Gossip columnist Louella Parsons declared that she was going to avoid the restaurant in order to resist the fattening desserts. In the 1930s, a fad "grapefruit diet" was popular among celebrities to lose weight, so Cobb told his chef to come up with a grapefruit cake and Parsons never left. However, the dessert was made with cream cheese frosting and so was actually higher in calories than the chocolate cake.

The restaurant became famous for its celebrity caricatures that decorated the walls. The earliest ones were drawn by Eddie Vitch beginning in 1931 in exchange for free meals. Other artists over the years included Zel, Pancho, Jack Lane (1947–1985), and Bunn.

For Disney fans, a framed photo near the restrooms shows Disney artist Herb Ryman doing a sketch of entertainer George Jessel. One of the caricatures in the lobby is of a mouse-eared Jimmie Dodd of the original *Mickey Mouse Club* television show. The brass derbies used as lampshades and other memorabilia add to the sense of authenticity.

Rock'n' Roller Coaster with Aerosmith

Aerosmith lead singer Steve Tyler said in July 1999:

> When you've toured the world as much as we have, it's a real thrill to find a new audience. Coming up with a soundtrack for this Disney ride really brought the kid out in all of us and has given us the opportunity to play audio gymnastics with our music.

Rock'n' Roller Coaster with Aerosmith opened at Disney's Hollywood Studios July 29, 1999. A steel roller coaster created by the Vekoma Rides Manufacturing company, it has powerful linear synchronous motors (LSM) that catapult the super-stretch limo vehicle (inspired by the design of a 1962 Cadillac) from 0–57 miles per hour in just 2.8 seconds into a giant cobra roll and later a corkscrew inversion.

Lead Designer Jim Shull stated:

> The idea behind the ride is that guests just stepped into a recording studio where Aerosmith is rehearsing for an awards show. Suddenly, the group's harried manager [actress Illeana Douglas] rushes in and announces that the band is running late. The members refuse to go to the show unless their loyal fans get to go as well.

> So, 24 guests at a time, we pile you, the fans, into an enormous stretch limo—and you're off.

To justify having such an attraction in an area themed to 1940s Hollywood, the Imagineers came up with an interesting storyline that neither the guests nor the cast ever adopted and has been largely ignored and forgotten.

The queue line is themed to G-Force records, a fictional record company that was supposedly started in the 1930s. (The intercom calls for people are the names of Imagineers who worked on the attraction.) G-Force was known for attracting the best of the best in recording artists and became a growing force in the industry.

Things took a turn for the worse on Halloween night 1939. While throwing a party at the neighboring Hollywood Tower Hotel (Twilight

Zone Tower of Terror), a strange incident occurred where lightning struck the building and five hotel guests mysteriously disappeared. The hotel was closed and the public felt that somehow G-Force was responsible and their record sales plummeted.

Over time G-Force as a business began to re-emerge and rebuilt the existing studio, adding a giant forty-foot Stratocaster as its icon. Today at G-Force many of the top recording stars can be found using the state-of-the-art facilities.

G-force (with the "g" from "gravitational") is a measurement of acceleration that causes the pressure of weight, such as during a rocket launch. The guests on the attraction experience 4.5 Gs, more than an astronaut does on a space shuttle launch.

Aerosmith band members Steve Tyler and Joe Perry rode the attraction twelve times in a row and made several changes primarily to the recording studio pre-show to make it more realistic, including the location of the guitars.

The vehicles have a built-in audio system that includes 125 speakers, 24 sub-woofers (under each seat), and more than 32k watts of audio amplifier output.

Each vehicle features a different Aerosmith song or medley. The tracks are: "Nine Lives", "Sweet Emotion", a "Back in the Saddle"/"Dude Looks Like a Lady" medley, a "Love in an Elevator"/"Walk This Way" medley, and a "Young Lust"/"F.I.N.E."/ "Love in an Elevator" medley. Tyler and Perry were involved in the re-recording of the songs, including changing the lyrics to "Love in an Elevator" to "Love in a Roller Coaster".

Aerosmith was chosen for the attraction because they were connected with Disney after having had supplied two songs ("I Don't Want to Miss a Thing" and "What Kind of Love Are You On") for the soundtrack album of the 1998 Touchstone Pictures film *Armageddon*. It was rumored that Disney first approached the Rolling Stones, but logistical and financial issues like paying a premium price for the rights to their songs derailed that deal.

Chinese Theater Handprints

The historic movie palace Grauman's Chinese Theater in Hollywood, California, may be best known for its forecourt filled with celebrity handprints and footprints that are pressed into concrete during a special ceremony.

When Disney-MGM Studios opened in May 1989, entertainment celebrities were invited to place their hand and foot prints into the concrete in the park's re-creation of that famous forecourt.

Disney instituted the Star Today program where a celebrity would appear at the park, often for a week, and participate in a motorcade, a public interview about their career, and a handprint ceremony.

The very first Star Today, on May 1, 1989, was original Mouseketeer Annette Funicello, and her concrete block is still in the forecourt. She only wrote her first name.

After 1995, the handprint ceremony still took place for publicity purposes, but the block was never installed in the forecourt. Actress Susan Lucci did multiple handprint ceremonies over different years as part of the ABC Super Soap weekend event.

It was expensive to rip up the existing concrete and install the new block and secure it. Over the years, some blocks have been damaged and removed but not replaced. Some imprinted blocks that were in storage were later installed in the forecourt of the Theater of the Stars on Sunset Boulevard.

There was no consistency. Some stars only wrote their names. Some did not date their block. Some included their family. Some put in only a handprint or only a footprint but not both.

George Lucas' connection with the Star Tours and Indiana Jones attractions at the park resulted in imprints from Lucas, Harrison Ford, Mark Hamill, and even C-3PO and R2-D2.

The courtyard is a mixture of stars from the Golden Age of films like Douglas Fairbanks Jr., June Allyson, and Donald O'Connor;

Disney characters like Mickey and Minnie Mouse, Goofy, Donald Duck, and Roger Rabbit; and more contemporary stars like Robin Williams, Tom Cruise, and Samuel L. Jackson.

Jim Henson's block was done on August 28, 1989, and also includes the signature of Kermit the Frog. Henson drew an illustration of Kermit's head and left hand waving. This was one of the few blocks actually done with the block already in place. Henson's own Kermit puppet's hands are imprinted.

Actress Daryl Hannah imprinted her bare feet and then drew the outline of a mermaid tail flippers around them as a reference to her role in the film *Splash* (1984).

The Rocketeer not only left his boot prints, but there are blast marks from his rocket pack behind his feet.

When actor Charlton Heston was signing his block, a fan called out the actor's name. Heston looked up briefly and was distracted, so he wrote "Charton" without the letter "l".

Steve Martin put in his handprints and then drew arrows to them and wrote the word "feet".

The ruby slippers that Judy Garland wore in the 1939 film *The Wizard of Oz* that were on loan for display in the attraction queue were carefully imprinted into a block.

Actor Sylvester Stallone put the name "Oscar" on his block referring to his character's name in the film he was working on at Disney-MGM Studios. Actor Warren Beatty put the initials "D.T." in parentheses because at the time he was starring as Dick Tracy in the movie of the same name.

Actress Loni Anderson made an impression that was so slight that when it rained her imprint quickly filled with water and guests would trip when walking over the block, so it was removed.

Sunset Boulevard Theaters

Sunset Boulevard was to showcase the theater district in Hollywood. Hollywood was notable for its many movie premieres and elaborate movie palaces like Grauman's Chinese Theater.

Starting at the top of the street, to the left is the Beverly Sunset shop with an exterior that looks like a movie theater. Its façade is based on the Warner Beverly Hills theater, a movie palace on Hollywood Boulevard that opened in 1931. The original theater was replaced by a parking lot in 1988.

When it first opened in 1994, the Beverly Sunset's interior was designed to be reminiscent of a movie theater. As guests enter, on the left is the concession counter and ticket stand (actually an opportunity to purchase some sweet treats and pay a cashier for purchases).

Lush curtains lead into the main theater and on the wall was a large screen showing Disney cartoons. Observant guests would notice the projector and items like film can reels above and opposite the screen. Some of the original trappings still exist on the walls today.

To the right, at the top of the street, is the Legends of Hollywood store. The exterior is inspired by the Academy Theater that was originally built to become the home of the annual Academy Awards ceremonies, but that never happened for a variety of reasons. However, it did exist as a movie theater from 1933 to 1975 when it became a church and is known today as the Academy Cathedral.

The reason the authentic 1941 gold-colored Cadillac touring sedan (Series 62 with its distinctive hood ornament) is out in front of the theater under a canopy is that it has pulled up to let some important people out for a premiere. Once upon a time, a red carpet went from the car to the entrance.

At the entrance to Legends of Hollywood is a ticket booth filled with authentic items, including actual coins and tickets from the time period just like the items in the station master's office on the second floor of the Main Street train station at the Magic Kingdom.

Reproductions of actual movie posters decorate the outside display cases and also set the time period. Inside the store is a hand-painted mural featuring all of the old movie theaters re-created at the park.

Nearby is the Planet Hollywood Super Store that also has a movie theater façade. It was inspired by the La Reina Theater in Sherman Oaks, California, that opened in 1937. Since the single-screen theater could not be transformed into a multi-screen space, it was sold in 1985 to a shopping center developer who planned to demolish it but met with opposition from preservationists.

While the theater auditorium was demolished in 1987, the theater's exterior façade was preserved but later damaged in a 1995 earthquake.

Unlike Legends of Hollywood, the theater posters that decorate the exterior of the store are fanciful creations of typical Hollywood movie genres. The poster that is an homage to science fiction movies includes the Planet Hollywood logo as part of its design.

The Once Upon a Time store has an exterior modeled after the famous Carthay Circle Theater that opened on San Vincente Boulevard in Los Angeles in 1926. The ornate theater hosted the premiere of such Disney films as the first Silly Symphony short, *Skeleton Dance* (1929), *Snow White and the Seven Dwarfs* (1937), and *Fantasia* (1940), as well as such classics films as *Gone with the Wind* (1939). It was torn down in 1969. The store is decorated with the film poster and framed black-and-white photos from the premiere of *Snow White*.

Beauty and the Beast Live on Stage

"Beauty and the Beast Live on Stage" premiered at 1:30pm on November 22, 1991, at Disney-MGM Studios, the same day that the popular animated film was released in the United States. This was the first and only time that a Disney theme park live-action show debuted on the exact same day as the official release of the film that inspired it.

The show was originally performed at the old Theater of the Stars stage located where the entrance to Sunset Boulevard exists today.

Its first stage show was entitled "Hollywood!" and featured songs and dances capturing the history of Hollywood movies but using Disney characters like Mickey and Minnie Mouse, Donald Duck, Pluto, and Goofy, as well as the "Disney Girls" dancers.

It was replaced in 1990 by "Dick Tracy Diamond Double Cross" to promote the recently released live-action feature film. In addition, two other shows, "Swing, Swing, Swing" and "Hollywood's Pretty Woman" (with a guest appearance at the end by Miss Piggy) ran concurrently during the day. In 1991, "Beauty and the Beast Live on Stage" began its now twenty-five-year run.

The show was briefly moved to the Backlot Theater in 1993 as construction work started on the Sunset Boulevard expansion. The show re-opened in the newly built 1,500 seat Theater of the Stars, meant to reference the iconic Hollywood Bowl amphitheater, in July 1994, where it has run ever since.

"Beauty and the Beast" is one of the longest continuously running shows at a Disney theme park, exceeded only by the "Hoop-Dee-Doo-Revue" and the "Golden Horseshoe Revue". Its success helped inspire the development of a full Broadway musical version.

The president of Walt Disney Theatrical Productions, Ron Logan, said in 2010:

> The stage shows at Walt Disney World gave us an opportunity to differentiate the brand of one park from the other. The success of

those shows, in particular our theme park live stage version of *Beauty and the Beast* at the Disney-MGM Studios and an additional version of *Beauty and the Beast* in a stage show at Disneyland sparked my interest in attempting to take the Disney stage show to the next level.

A new opportunity evolved, the opportunity of producing what we call a "live attraction". A live attraction is a stage show in essence which uses live entertainment and entertainment industry technology to produce live shows, short in length, that can be performed many times in a day. We evolved a formula for live attraction-based shows on the success of the first shows we produced.

The original Florida show was revised in March 2001 to more closely resemble the running order of the animated film and establish a clearer story beginning, middle, and end. This revision included a new prologue and has been performed ever since that time.

The roughly twenty-five-minute production is an abridged version of the story but captures the highlights on the classic animated feature, although some favorite scenes and characters are missing.

Pre-recorded tracks of vocal performances by Robby Benson as the Beast, Angela Lansbury as Mrs. Potts, Jerry Orbach as Lumière, David Ogden Stiers as Cogsworth, and Bradley Pierce as Chip the cup are used in the show. The actress playing Belle and the actor playing Gaston both speak and sing in their own voices.

In 1985, Disneyland had an entertainment space named Videopolis that served as a music-and-dance venue, especially in the evenings. It featured seventy monitors playing music videos. In 1989, it was converted into a stage theater and ran a significantly different and more elaborate live-action version of *Beauty and the Beast* from April 1992 to April 1995. In 1995, the venue was renamed the Fantasyland Theater.

Disneyland Paris used the Florida production script and staging for a *Beauty and the Beast* live-action show that ran at its Videopolis Theater from 1992 through 1996.

Kali River Rapids

The Asia area opened at Disney's Animal Kingdom in 1999 and included the popular water ride Kali River Rapids.

Just as Walt Disney originally wanted live animals on the Jungle Cruise at Disneyland, Imagineers initially developed an attraction called Tiger Rapids Run for DAK. The attraction would be a water safari on large raft-like vehicles giving guests a different view of the tiger habitat as well as encounters with other animals before finishing by shooting the rapids and a drop that felt "like the bottom has dropped out of the river", according to project director Joe Rohde.

There are still examples of tigers in the final attraction, including multiple references in the queue line as well as carved images on top of the wooden pagoda where guests board the rafts. Of course, the final animal stone sentinel at the top of the ninety-foot lift at the beginning of the ride is a tiger at the entrance to Tiger Bay.

Even though it was planned as a much longer ride than the version that was finally built, Imagineers decided that because of the speed of the attraction, guests might only see animals for fleeting seconds and that the noise and movement from the guests and the vehicles might disturb the animals.

So the attraction was changed into a botanical expedition where guests could enjoy the scenic beauty of the forest and then be shocked at how it is being ravaged and burned by illegal logging, just as Africa's Kilimanjaro Safaris told the story of the dangers of poaching. Basically, the ride became an ecotourism experience with the sound of wildlife coming from hidden speakers.

All of this is explained in a voice-over during the queue line by the fictional owner:

> Hello, my name is Manisha Gurung. I am the founder and manager of Kali Rapids Expeditions. When you board one of our rafts, you can look forward to an exciting, safe and very wet trip down a stretch

of beautiful river. My team and I believe that our river rides are more than just an exciting adventure. We believe they help spread a message to visitors about preserving wild places. Like our forest.

All around Anandapur, logging companies in search of tropical hardwood have bitten deep into the jungle. When this happens, the traditional life of the village and forest is destroyed forever. I created this river rafting experience to demonstrate that there are nondestructive ways to bring revenue to the village because the more people like you care, the better chance our jungle has of surviving. Thanks for choosing Kali Rapids Expeditions. We hope your journey will show you a world that is truly worth saving.

Guring and her family live in a house elevated on stilts near the entrance of the attraction. Since Guring is busy elsewhere, she fails to hear that the logging has gotten too close to the river so is not there to stop guests from being dispatched.

Kali River Rapids was manufactured by Intamin (INTernational AMusement INstallations), a Swiss company noted for thrill rides and roller coasters. It built the very first "river rapids ride", Thunder River, for AstroWorld in 1980. The company was also responsible for Grizzly River Run at Disney's California Adventure in 2001.

Each circular raft with colorful individual names like Sherpa Surfer, Kali Bumper Car, and Manaslu Slammer seat twelve people around the perimeter as geysers, waterfalls, statues of water carriers, and squirting elephants soak the guests.

The bobbing up and down and spinning journey goes down the Chakranadi meaning the "river that flows in a circle" in Sanskrit which is why the rafts return to the same place they disembarked. The name Kali refers to the Hindu Goddess of destruction, referencing the smoldering charred tree trunks that originally featured fire effects.

Be warned that no matter what precautions you take, you will get wet but you MIGHT get soaked, depending upon the twists and turns of fate.

Kilimanjaro Safaris

According to the official back story when Disney Animal Kingdom first opened:

> Kilimanjaro Safaris is just one of many companies that offers photo excursions to tourists from around the world to The Harambe Wildlife Reserve. After three decades of operation, it has emerged as the premier provider of safe, affordable animal-viewing safaris in their fleet of "Tembo" (Swahili for elephant) open-sided vehicles. In addition, the company hires and trains its safari drivers to offer a high level of information about the animals found on the Reserve.

Just as CEO Robert Iger's game plan for Disney expansion was to purchase popular franchises like Marvel and Lucasfilms, CEO Michael Eisner's game plan for Walt Disney World was to create entertainment that mimicked already popular offerings in the central Florida area to keep money spent by Disney guests on Disney property.

Busch Gardens Tampa opened in 1959 as an African-themed experience that grew to be one of the largest zoological institutions, with over 2,700 animals. In 1965, the park opened the twenty-nine acre Serengeti Plains, which allowed the African wildlife to roam freely. Its popularity encouraged Eisner to approve DAK.

One of the centerpieces for DAK would be the Kilimanjaro Safaris attraction, since guests would be eager to see animals differently than at a zoo. It is around 110 acres, making it roughly the size of the Magic Kingdom.

In July 1990, Imagineering creative director Joe Rohde took a team to Kenya and Tanzania for two weeks. They took thousands of photographs and countless hours of video. In addition, they participated in many family-owned safaris to try to understand what a typical tourist might experience on their first time making such a visit.

Landscape architect Phil Schenkel along with senior project engineer Dave Dahlke had to devise a recipe for concrete for the

Kilimanjaro Safaris' two miles of rutted, potholed, and washed out "dirt" road. They spent long hours matching the concrete color with the surrounding soil and then rolled tires through it as well as tossed stones, dirt, and twigs to capture a seamless sense of reality not immediately recognized by the guests.

In addition, the roadway was designed to keep any water in the path separate from the water used by the animals. The potholes in the road with water actually have their own pumping and drainage system.

The Imagineers set up a test track in the parking lot at WDI in Glendale with similar potholes and ruts. However, when they took Disney executive Marty Sklar for a practice spin, he spilled most of his coffee and his instant displeasure resulted in them going back to the drawing board to modify the design.

The ride still ended up pretty bumpy when it first opened with the park and some adjustments were made, including additional padding on the backs of the seats.

Some factors in selecting the animals to be exhibited included if they would be active during the day, could be easily contained, got along well with the other selected animals, and how they would react to the tourists. Zoologist Rick Barongi provided input.

Originally, to emphasize the park's commitment to conservation, the attraction included a story about the dangers of illegal poachers with signage, urgent radio alerts, and more. The guests were involved in a frantic chase to rescue a kidnapped elephant named Big Red and her baby, Little Red.

That storyline with game warden Wilson Mutua and the beloved elephants was both upsetting and confusing to guests and was redone as surveys showed guests were primarily interested in spotting live animals.

McDonald's and DAK

In January 1997, McDonald's entered into a ten year agreement with the Disney company for promotions of Disney films, videos, TV properties, and theme parks.

Disney allowed McDonald's to open six food locations in the four Disney parks as well as actual fast food restaurants at Walt Disney World's Downtown Disney and another near Disney's All-Star Resorts.

At Disney's Hollywood Studios, McDonald's sponsored Fairfax Fries at the Sunset Ranch Market. Fairfax is a reference to the street where the famous Los Angeles Farmers Market (the inspiration for the Sunset Ranch Market) is located.

At Epcot, at the entrance to the World Showcase promenade, McDonald's handled the Refreshment Port where sometimes international cast members from Canada brought Canadian Smarties (a candy similar to American M&Ms) for the food and beverage location to make a Smarties McFlurry. Not only were custom McFlurries available but also Chicken McNuggets and French fries.

McDonald's Fry Cart serving French fries and soft drinks opened in Magic Kingdom's Frontierland in 1999.

As part of the arrangement, McDonald's agreed to sponsor the entire DinoLand section of Animal Kingdom that opened in 1998. Everything from the Dino Institute with the Countdown to Extinction attraction to the Boneyard to Restaurantosaurus were branded by McDonald's.

In fact, Restaurantosaurus offered a fuller McDonald's menu than at other park locations but renamed items as Dino-Sized Double Cheeseburger and Hot Dog-osaurus. In the Happy Meals, the toys were T-Rex, Stegosaurus, Pterodactyl, and Triceratops water pistols.

The Restaurantosaurus back story is that it was a student commissary in a building that also served as a dormitory and classroom.

During McDonald's tenure in the area, there were two signs illustrated by famed dinosaur artist William Stout. One featured a T-Rex gobbling down a smaller dinosaur and the slogan "Have you had a Crocodilian today?" to parody McDonald's slogan of "Have you had a break today?"

The second sign was a mock movie poster for a dinosaur-on-the-loose-in-modern-times film entitled *It Came Through the Drive-Thru*. Starring Hap P. Meal, Hanover D. Fries, and I. C. McNuggets. Produced by Gordon Arches and Presented by Prehistoric Pictures.

To promote the park nationally, McDonald's Animal Kindom Happy Meal featured twelve animal toys. There was a Triceratops, toucan, gorilla (with her baby), elephant, lemur, dragon (that flapped its wings), Iguanodon, zebra, lion, cheetah, crocodile, tortoise, and rhino. They all had different actions such as the gorilla spinning her baby, the zebra being a wind-up toy, and the tortoise sticking his head in and out of his shell.

The purple, fire-breathing dragon intended for the never-built Beastly Kingdom was not just a toy but appeared on Happy Meal boxes and on beverage cups.

For Japan and other countries, McDonald's released a set of four Happy Meals figures not available in the United States: Minnie Mouse with a baby gorilla from Gorilla Falls Exploration Trail, Mickey Mouse in a Kilimanjaro Safaris jeep, Goofy digging for fossils with an Iguanodon, and Donald Duck in a Discovery River Boat.

While Disney netted more than $100 million dollars in royalties during the decade-long agreement, McDonald's netted more than $1 billion from the deal, which included promoting Disney's box office bombs like *Dinosaur* (2000), *Atlantis: The Lost Empire* (2001), *Treasure Planet* (2002), and *Home on the Range* (2004).

McDonald's promotion for a film might exceed Disney's budget for advertising, so in addition to the royalty money, Disney got additional visibility for its films. However, the agreement prevented McDonald's from promoting non-Disney films in its franchises and that helped sour the relationship.

Restaurantosaurus

The DinoLand section of Disney's Animal Kingdom was intended to reflect the American love of dinosaurs, from serious scientific discovery to tacky roadside attractions. It was also meant to tell the story of the conflict between the youthful disobedience and prankster nature of graduate students versus the more stodgy and controlling nature of adult authority.

Both of these story elements are reflected in Restaurantosaurus.

When the park opened in 1998, the restaurant was operated by McDonald's as part of an extensive ten-year sponsorship agreement with Disney. When McDonald's decided not to renew, the restaurant reverted to Disney and items that referenced McDonald's were removed.

The back story is that the building was originally a quiet, remote fishing lodge along U.S. Highway 498 (DAK opened in April 1998) in Diggs County, roughly fifty miles away from the nearest town.

In 1947, an amateur fossil hunter found a few old bones near the lodge. Later, his paleontologist friends confirmed that he had discovered a major scientific find. They bought the lodge and much of the surrounding land to begin their excavations.

The professors and their grad students took up residence in the lodge and converted it into an ever-expanding dormitory. Needing more funds to support their work, the student commissary was opened up to curious tourists who had come to visit the Boneyard dig site. Since it was originally meant for college students, the menu offered predominantly fast food.

A simple sign stating "Restaurant" was erected. The prankster nature of the students is apparent in their adding the dinosaur inspired suffix "osaurus" to the sign and other signs in the area, such as Bunk Room-osaurus and Vehicle Maintenance-osaurus.

The building also evolved into a tourist information visitor center and later a small museum displaying some of the artifacts that had been unearthed. The need for a larger support facility became evident and a Quonset hut for vehicle maintenance was added adjacent to the lodge.

Later expansions included the plastering room, the auxiliary storage shed, some additional tented buildings, and the recreation room nicknamed "The Hip Joint". Each of these dining areas is packed with story details.

Tributes to Walt Disney himself include a photo of him with the audio-animatronics dinosaurs for the 1964–65 New York World's Fair and reproductions of model sheets from the "Rite of Spring" segment from the animated feature film *Fantasia* (1940).

The building became the first home of the Dino Institute and classes were offered. When the trustees hired Dr. Helen Marsh to increase cash flow, she purchased Chrono-Tech Inc. and announced that the newly invented Time Rover technology would be available to the general public. This influx in money and additional funding allowed a new state-of-the-art facility for research and classes to be built.

The restaurant is purposely a messy jumble of chaos because the students living there are too busy to be bothered by appearances. Many amusing touches decorate the area, including student awards given to their peers over the years.

The Zip award went to the student who worked the hardest and had gotten nothing or "zip" to show for it. The Golden Trowel award goes to the student with the most discoveries over the year. The Golden Boot award went to the intern that walked the most miles in search of bones.

A guest can spend hours tracing the intricate back story through the various rooms, including finding cans of Sinclair Oil, the brand sold at Chester and Hester's former gas station before those "dinosaurs" set up shop themselves nearby with amusement-type games and rides.

It's Tough to Be a Bug

Many different proposals were considered for the area at the base of Animal Kingdom's Tree of Life. At one point, the area would have been used by The Roots Restaurant, an upscale eatery. When it was decided the area should feature a show, a Wonders of Nature and a Lion King character show were possibilities that were seriously discussed.

CEO Michael Eisner suggested during a particularly disappointing pitch meeting that bugs live in and under trees and that Pixar Animation was working on a new feature film about bugs called *A Bug's Life* (1998). Imagineering consulted directly with Pixar. While several characters from the film were used, new ones were created as well.

The decision to go with this concept was approved after construction had already begun on the Tree of Life. However, it still opened in April 1998, roughly a full seven months before the release of the film that inspired it.

The queue line into the theater was designed to create the illusion that guests were shrinking to bug size as they navigated the increasingly narrow tunnels with everything else including the roots seeming to become enormous.

The nine-minute show being performed in the 430-seat auditorium—It's Tough To Be A Bug! Starring Flik and a cast of A Million Billion Bugs—is similar to a vaudeville revue with individual acts.

This performance is the current show produced by the Tree of Life Repertory Theater. The pre-show waiting lobby is decorated with playbill posters from past performances whose titles are parodies of popular Broadway shows. Over the years, the followings posters were displayed:

- My Fair Ladybug (*My Fair Lady*)
- Barefoot in the Bark (Neil Simon's *Barefoot in the Park*)
- A Grass Menagerie (Tennessee Williams' *A Glass Menagerie*)

- A Cockroach Line (*A Chorus Line*)
- Beauty and the Bees: "Bee Our Guest!" (Disney's *Beauty and the Beast*)
- Antie (*Annie*)
- Web Side Story (*West Side Story*)
- Little Shop of Hoppers (*Little Shop of Horrors*)
- A Stinkbug Named Desire (*A Streetcar Named Desire*)
- The Dung and I, featuring the hit song "Hello Dung Lovers" (*The King and I*).

Some of the poster designs were done by Imagineers Nicole Armitage Doolittle (daughter of Frank Armitage, a Disney animation background artist and later Imagineer) and Milton Noji (who worked for almost five years at Disney on both interior and exterior signage). Unlike traditional theater posters, these posters are not decorated with snippets of critics' reviews but interesting facts about the insect world.

The background music consists of a bug orchestra, sounding a lot like buzzing kazoos, playing iconic songs from these shows

- "One" (*Chorus Line*)
- "Beauty and the Beast" (*Beauty and the Beast*)
- "Tomorrow" (*Annie*)
- "I Feel Pretty" (*West Side Story*)
- "Hello Young Lovers" (*The King and I*)
- "Tonight" (*West Side Story* but also includes the counterpoint "Flight of the Bumblebee").

The theme song, "It's Tough to be a Bug", was written by George Wilkins with lyrics by Kevin Rafferty (the show writer for the project). The show's score was composed and conducted by Bruce Broughton. Rafferty, after meeting with insect naturalist Ray Mendez, said:

> My job was to impart the facts about ten quintillion bugs in only eight minutes. Ray said that, most important, they are responsible for our food, as pollinators, and they handle our waste. If it weren't for bugs, we'd all be dead in six months. That impressed me. All the acts featured in the show are based on what actual bugs do. There really, truly are acid-spraying termites.

DINOSAUR

DINOSAUR opened as Countdown to Extinction at DinoLand in April 1998, and is one of the few Disney theme park attractions that opened before the release of the movie that inspired it.

After Disney's animated film *Dinosaur* was released in May 2000, the attraction was renamed to the movie title. The logo on the building was taken down and replaced with a sign featuring the logo for the film. The original statue at the front of the building, a Styracosaurus, was replaced with a statue of Aladar, the Iguanodon hero of the film.

In the attraction, guests board vehicles called Time Rovers at the Dino Institute and are sent to the Cretaceous period that contains several elements from the film, including the appearance of a Carnotaurus, Igaunodon, and a meteor shower.

Realizing that the newly named attraction might attract a younger audience that had seen the movie, the movement of the vehicles was changed to be less intense and the soundtrack was revised to be less frightening so that the sound of the Carnotaurus seemed farther in the distance.

Imagineer Joe Rohde, executive designer of Disney's Animal Kingdom, and other Imagineers involved in the creation of the park worked closely with the Walt Disney Pictures team that created *Dinosaur* to create the unique ride experience.

To publicize the film, there were even plans to have an audio-animatronics dinosaur parade down Main Street at Disneyland. Those readers who saw the 2012 Travel Channel special on Imagineering saw a huge box drop open and a free standing four-legged audio-animatronics dinosaur take a few steps.

Those experiments in the "Living Character Initiative" evolved into Lucky, the dinosaur prototype for the next generation of audio-animatronics figures. At 20-feet long and roughly 12-feet tall, the 450-pound Lucky, who smiles, grunts, sneezes, bats his eyelashes, and signs clover-shaped autographs, had successful test runs at Disney's California Adventure and later at Disney's Animal Kingdom.

Lucky is patterned after the Gallimimus dinosaur, but Disney designers took some liberties to soften his image so children of all ages would fall in love with him. He did vocalizations including hiccups.

Lucky was five years in development. Unlike earlier animatronics figures, Lucky is operated by electric motors and sensors that are controlled through a central computer, which regulates everything from Lucky's ponderous footsteps to the gentle batting of his eyelashes. The batteries and computer were located in the flower cart that he pulled.

The type of skin generally used for other animatronics characters could not be used for Lucky because it was too heavy, so Imagineers developed a lighter, more flexible skin.

Lucky was also meant to publicize the four-hour television mini-series *Dinotopia* (2002) which is why Lucky's "handler" who walked along his side was attired in garb appropriate for that show.

Lucky's first appearance was at the Natural History Museum of Los Angeles on August 28, 2003. A few days later he visited Disney's California Adventure.

Since Lucky was only "play testing", he returned to his home at Walt Disney Imagineering and eventually made appearances in Disney's Animal Kingdom (May 6, 2005) and Hong Kong Disneyland.

Today, he's back home at Walt Disney Imagineering and makes occasional appearances for Adventures by Disney guests, the D23 2009 Expo, and non-Disney events like the 2008 World Science Festival.

Horticulture

When Animal Kingdom opened in 1998, it required over four million plants including everything from huge trees to the smallest shoots of grass. There were 46,202 Vetiver grass shoots planted by opening day. The number of species of grass exceeded three hundred. Just in the Africa area, more than 771,687 shrubs and nearly 70,000 trees were planted.

Suppliers were contacted all over the United States and arrangements were made for plants to be propagated in temperate zones in California, Florida, Arizona, and Maryland before being shipped to the site.

A "heritage area" was created on the berm so that trees and plants there could replace plants in the park when they died.

A "browse farm" of acacia, hibiscus, and bamboo was set up to provide food for the leaf-eating animals. While the different species of hoof stock may choose different plant species on which to feed, their diet is not solely dependent on African plant species. All of the animals receive supplemental nutritionally balanced diets to help maintain good health.

This browse farm and outside vendors produce thousands of pounds of cut browse weekly. It is positioned throughout the animal habitats such as the savannas for the animals to feed on, which in turn reduces the impact on the planted landscape.

One of the landscape designers, Michelle Sullivan, recalled:

> Okapi, a rare and beautiful cousin of the giraffe, eat everything so I have to spend hours scouring plant lists to see if any are toxic or there is any vegetation classified as "noxious weeds" that means a species that might grow out of control in Florida's lush landscape.

Unlike the previous Disney theme parks, it was plants, not buildings and facades, that dominated the storytelling. A staff of eight landscape architects who had all being taught by Bill Evans (the man responsible for landscaping Disneyland, Magic Kingdom, and Epcot Center) accomplished the never-before-done challenge.

In August 1996, principal landscape architect Paul Comstock said:

> In Animal Kingdom, the design challenge facing us is to help tell the story, the natural story. Landscape becomes the show in many areas. It is awesome. It is the set. It is the show.

Over a five-year period, Comstock visited Madagascar, South Africa, Kenya, Tanzania, Tasmania, Namibia, China, Thailand, Indonesia, and Singapore collecting seeds and shoots and establishing relationships with nurseries and botanical gardens. Material was gathered from every continent on Earth, except for Antarctica.

Ancient cycads, survivors of the Cretaceous Period and over sixty-seven million years old, that were needed for the DinoLand area were found in Florida and from a collector in Eagle Rock, California.

Landscape architecture manager Carl Walsten said that one of the important things he learned from landscape consultant Bill Evans was that:

> There's not one perfect answer. A red flowering tree might be one of several available, but we also need to understand whether that plant works in our micro-climate. That's where Bill's knowledge is so valuable. You don't learn this in school, but from experience.
>
> We even joke about our "new species of acacia", the characteristic flat-topped trees that dot the real African savanna. The mature Animal Kingdom "acacias" are in reality conserved thirty-foot-tall oak trees with "crew cuts" that mimic the African trees.

An example of a look-alike would be the use of *Enterolobium cyclocarpa* to represent large "fever trees". Disney planted the actual fever tree, *Acacia xanthophloea,* on the savannas, but they rarely reached maximum size in the central Florida climate and so were not "good show".

As with many details at Disney theme parks, it is the illusion of reality more than authenticity that guarantees that guests will become immersed in the overall experience.

The Forbidden Mountain

Expedition Everest—Legend of the Forbidden Mountain opened at Disney's Animal Kingdom in 2006. The mountain-like structure is made from 1,800 tons of steel and painted with 2,000 gallons of stain and paint. It took three years and more than 38 miles of rebar, 5,000 tons of structural steel, and 10,000 tons of concrete to build the mountain. Over 200,000 square feet of rock work was done

The structure was built by Vekoma, a Dutch amusement ride manufacturer noted for its work on roller coasters including ones for Disney theme parks like the recent Seven Dwarfs Mine Train in the Magic Kingdom.

The total cost for the attraction was estimated at over $100 million. It is the tallest artificial mountain in the world at 199 feet but not the tallest mountain in Florida which is Britton Hill at 345 feet.

The Forbidden Mountain is not Everest. Everest is represented by the barren background peak on the far right that through the use of forced perspective seems off in the distance.

Guests are on an expedition to Everest on an old mountain railroad operated by the fictional Himalayan Escapes—Tours and Expeditions company but are taking a risky shortcut through the Forbidden Mountain to get to the Everest base camp. The attraction has nearly a mile-long length of track that encompasses steep climbs, sharp plunges, and a backward slide.

Imagineer Joe Rohde, the executive designer of the attraction, said in 2007:

> The name of our story is Expedition Everest, but nothing in the shape of the real Everest says "forbidden". So we created the narrative device of a foreground mountain range made of shapes that say, "Don't go here!"
>
> Everest rises beyond this wall of claw-like spires, a tempting goal. The forbidden mountain expresses its "forbidden-ness" in a shape that echoes the teeth and claws of the Yeti itself, dominating the

entire land across which the story plays out. This is one of the key principles in narrative placemaking.

The look of Expedition Everest is based on careful research into the architecture, landscape and culture of the Himalayas: research and design guided by our theme. Our goal was not to create a replica, nor to represent every aspect of Himalayan life, but to gather those specific details which were both authentic and supported the thrust of our theme, the intrinsic value of nature.

Expedition Everest is not meant to be a substitute for a trip to the real Himalayas; it is a fictional story told in a realistic style.

While the environment is visually convincing and filled with accurate details, including architectural elements and props made for us by craftspeople in the Himalayas, its real purpose is to convey messages. The idea of the Yeti as a protector is embedded in shrines depicting the Yeti holding the mountains in his hands, bronzes of the Yeti in the traditional "keep out" posture of a Tibetan guardian, flyers printed from wood blocks warning visitors against offending the Yeti.

The Imagineers who designed the mountain used digital imaging to create a model. They created 24 different ride models before settling on the one that was built. They created a virtual model after scanning one of their earlier models with laser technology. The shell of the mountain was created digitally into six-foot square pieces that fit together like puzzle pieces.

Rohde continued:

Millions have ridden it. Most of those have come for the simple fun of a great ride. But of those millions, some have come away inspired and informed by the richness of the story. And as a percentage of the huge total, that number is also large.

PART TWO

The Walt Disney World Resorts

Before Walt Disney World opened in October 1971, the Orlando area offered about 5,800 hotel and motel rooms. By June 1972, that total had jumped to around 10,000 rooms with another 7,000 more rooms under construction.

During the first year of WDW operation, hotels and motels were booked solid with tourists sometimes being diverted to Tampa and Daytona Beach for lodging (and an additional hour's drive back to Walt Disney World via hotel shuttle bus).

Today, for a guest to stay one night in each of the Disney resort rooms on property would take approximately seventy years. As of 2015, the number of rooms available in each Disney resort are:

- Disney's Contemporary Resort: 656 rooms
- Bay Lake Tower at Disney's Contemporary Resort: 294 two-bedroom equivalent villas (DVC)
- Disney's Grand Floridian Resort & Spa: 867 rooms
- The Villas at Disney's Grand Floridian Resort & Spa: 100 2-bedroom equivalent villas (DVC)
- Disney's Polynesian Village Resort: 484 rooms
- Disney's Polynesian Villas and Bungalows: 380 rooms (DVC)
- Disney's Wilderness Lodge: 727 rooms
- The Villas at Disney's Wilderness Lodge: 116 two-bedroom equivalent villas (DVC)
- Disney's Fort Wilderness Resort and Campground: 799 campsites and 408 cabins

- Disney's Caribbean Beach Resort: 2,109 rooms
- Disney's Yacht Club Resort: 621 rooms
- Disney's Beach Club Resort: 574 rooms
- Disney's Beach Club Villas: 172 two-bedroom equivalent villas (DVC)
- Disney's BoardWalk Inn: 372 rooms
- Disney's BoardWalk Villas: 279 two-bedroom equivalent villas (DVC)
- Disney's Port Orleans Resort–French Quarter—1,008 rooms
- Disney's Port Orleans Resort–Riverside: 2,047 rooms
- Disney's Old Key West Resort: 531 two-bedroom equivalent villas (DVC)
- Disney's Saratoga Springs Resort & Spa: 724 two-bedroom equivalent villas (DVC)
- Disney's Art of Animation Resort: 864 rooms, 1,120 suites
- Disney's Pop Century Resort: 2,870 rooms
- Disney's Animal Kingdom Lodge: 970 rooms
- Disney's Animal Kingdom Lodge Villas: 449 two-bedroom equivalent villas (DVC)
- Disney's Coronado Springs Resort: 1,912 rooms
- Disney's All-Star Movies Resort: 1,920 rooms
- Disney's All-Star Music Resort: 1,704 rooms
- Disney's All-Star Sports Resort: 1,920 rooms

The 1988 Opening

Newspaper advertisements in the summer of 1988 for Disney's Grand Floridian proclaimed:

> Journey back to the turn-of-the century...to another time and another place. The Grand Floridian Beach Resort. An oasis of elegance that's the first of its kind since the golden age of pleasure travel. Bright white towers and gabled roofs echo the Victorian architectural influence that has come to symbolize Florida's carefree winters and balmy summer nights.

Disney held a special press event June 23–26 that brought in 1,400 members of the media to celebrate the latest additions to Walt Disney World including Mickey's Birthdayland, the Norway Pavilion's Maelstrom attraction, Mickey's 60th birthday, and new production at Disney-MGM Studios.

In addition, it was the official dedication of the Grand Floridian Resort that opened July 1, 1988. CEO Michael Eisner and actor Burt Reynolds cut the ceremonial ribbon stretched between two palm trees to open the resort. An aquatic ballet was performed in the 275,000 gallon pool. Singers and dancers performed a medley of turn-of-the-century tunes.

Burt was honored by Disney as a "grand" Floridian at a gala dinner that night because of his many connections to the state. He was actually on WDW property to tape a segment of the game show that he co-produced, *Win, Lose or Draw*, being filmed at Disney-MGM Studios.

The Grand Floridian was inspired by the Victorian-era beach resorts built along Florida's east coast during the late 19th and early 20th centuries when wealthy and famous people from the north would travel by train to warmer climes.

The exterior is noticeably influenced by the iconic Hotel del Coronado in Coronado, California, with red gabled roofs and white walls. However, design elements were also taken from the Mount

Washington Resort in Bretton Woods, New Hampshire; the Grand Hotel on Mackinac Island, Michigan; and the Belleview-Biltmore Hotel in Bellair, Florida.

The Belleview Hotel, as it was initially known, was constructed by railroad tycoon Henry B. Plant in 1897 as a resort destination to boost tourist travel on the railroad line he had acquired in 1893 and which served the west coast of Florida. The hotel closed in 2009 and was demolished in 2015.

Mizner's Lounge was named after Addison Mizner, an architect who specialized in "Gatsby-esque" mansions in Palm Beach and Boca Raton.

The architecture of the Grand Floridian is a collage of American, English, French, and Caribbean. Rather than a historically accurate Victorian color theme that would have been too dark and somber for this playful seaside resort, the Imagineers selected soft greens, blues, and peaches.

Of particular interest, 1900 Park Fare restaurant features Big Bertha, an antique band organ built in Paris by Gavoli & Co at the turn of the century. After acquiring the organ, Disney installed it in an alcove fifteen feet above Park Fare guests. It plays music through a system of pipes, drums, castanets, bells, cymbals, and xylophone (originally, its music was played by means of paper piano-roll "books").

The organ was used from 1909 to 1955 in Ramona Park, an amusement park in Grand Rapids, Michigan, known as the Amusement Mecca of Western Michigan. The park was demolished in 1955 and the three antique band organs used for the merry-go-round went into storage in Alabama for many years where they were discovered in 1963 and restored.

The Grand Floridian Resort and Spa is a showcase of amazing details, from the Chinese-style aviary in the lobby that was crafted in Spain and the vintage Victorian piano in the lobby obtained from an estate in Georgia to the entrance of Victoria & Albert's that features eleven original maps of Florida dated from 1775 up to the period of railroad tycoon Henry M. Flagler's railway lines in the late 1880s.

Hoop-Dee-Doo Musical Revue

"Hoop-de-doo", a variant of "whoop-de-doo", is an old-fashioned expression meaning frenzied activity or excitement. That phrase became the cornerstone of one of Walt Disney World's most beloved nighttime entertainment experiences, the Hoop-Dee-Doo Musical Revue.

The show opened June 14, 1974, and continues to be performed in Pioneer Hall at the Fort Wilderness Resort and Campground to this day. It was inspired by the success of the South Seas Luau at the Polynesian Village Resort and the need to find a project for the Walt Disney World Fine Arts College Workshop that supplied an inexpensive and eager cast for the new show.

With music developed by Robert Jani, Ron Miziker, Tom Adair, Paul Suter, and Larry Billman, the show was a highly collaborative effort, including contributions from the original performers. Billman was the director and Forrest Bahruth was the choreographer.

The premise of the show is that the stagecoach of performers on their way to another engagement (an actual stagecoach used to be positioned outside of Pioneer Hall to support that storyline) had broken down. They come inside the dining hall to entertain while their stagecoach is being repaired and the guests enjoy an all-you-can-eat meal of fried chicken, ribs, strawberry shortcake, and other country fare between the corn-pone vaudeville acts.

Fort Wilderness Resort and Campground opened on November 19, 1971. When Pioneer Hall officially opened on April 1, 1974, it was called the Fort Wilderness Dining Hall. The area was intended to be used as a dining venue for breakfast and lunch as an extension of the adjacent Crockett's Tavern.

The original plans were that at night there would be lectures about and demonstrations by animals brought over from nearby Discovery Island. Guests would also be able to play games and perhaps enjoy some musical talent like a washboard band. In addition, a huge screen would show some of the True-Life Adventures documentary films made by the Disney studio in the 1950s and 1960s.

Built with 1,283 hand-fitted Western white pine logs from Montana and 70 tons of rare ebony stone from North Carolina for its pillars, the two-story building was modeled after a Northwest Territory Lodge from the late 1800s.

Walt Disney World had no expectations for the show other than trying to temporarily fill an operational need. In fact, many people involved in the show felt it would be cancelled in the first few weeks or after its initial eleven weeks when the students returned to school.

By the end of summer, it was such an unqualified success that the roles were staffed with professional performers beginning September 5, 1974.

Over the years, a few changes have been made in the original show. For instance, in the beginning and until 1979, it was apple pie and not strawberry shortcake that was served as dessert. As a result, the song "Apple Pie Hoedown" was replaced with "Strawberry Short Cake Walk".

However, the most significant change happened in 2011. The song "Hoop-Dee-Doo" (sometimes called the "Hoop-Dee-Doo Polka") used in the show was composed by Milton DeLugg with lyrics by Frank Loesser, and was first published in 1950. When the song was used in the Hoop-Dee-Doo Revue, the lyrics were rewritten to reflect the show, but the upbeat tune remained intact.

The only problem was that in the rush to put together a temporary patchwork show, it had not occurred to anyone at Disney to get proper clearance for the use of the song. When the situation came to light, during the late summer of 2011, the popular theme song was replaced with one written specifically for Disney that still included the phrase Hoop-De-Doo.

The Tri-Circle-D Ranch

On Main Street, USA at the Magic Kingdom, on the side of the car barn, is a window that honors "Owen Pope. Harness Maker".

Pope and his wife Dolly lived at Disneyland where they trained and cared for the horses. Their house is still located in the park behind Big Thunder Ranch and will be moved before the building of Star Wars Land. It was in this house that Owen made the harnesses and riggings for the horses that would work at Walt Disney World. That's why his window states "Harness Maker".

The Popes were relocated to Florida in January 1971, where they supervised the creation of the Tri-Circle-D Ranch at Fort Wilderness. Tri-Circle refers to the three circles that make the famous Mickey Mouse head silhouette and, of course, "D" stands for "Disney".

The Popes retired in 1975 but continued to visit at least once a year until their deaths. Owen died in 2000 at the age of 96, Dolly in 2003 at 89.

The Tri-Circle-D Ranch has two sections located roughly a mile apart. Horseback riding takes place at the Trail Blaze Corral just inside the main entrance of Disney's Fort Wilderness Resort and Campground, next to the Outpost area. Guests can take the reins for a 45-minute guided trail ride through the resort.

The remaining Tri-Circle-D Ranch areas with the draft horse barn, blacksmith shop, carriage rides, and pony rides (the ponies are adults and weigh on average 500 pounds; pony riders have to weigh less than 80 pounds and be under 48 inches tall) are located at the Settlement area, next to Pioneer Hall at the rear of the campground.

The draft horse barn has a small one-room museum named "Walt Disney Horses". It is a tribute to Walt Disney's love of horses, and decorated with photos and memorabilia.

Across from it is the 1907 Dragon Calliope housed under protective glass. Besides being part of the short-lived Mickey Mouse Club Circus parade in 1955, the calliope went on to appear at Disneyland parades until the park's 25th anniversary. It was then repainted silver and blue and relocated to Florida for the Walt Disney World Tencennial Celebration in 1981, where it has remained.

Generally, 80–90 horses are maintained at the ranch and roughly thirty of them are draft horses. The draft horses can get as large as 18 hands tall (72 inches). A hand is about four inches and was originally based on the breadth of a human hand as a measure. They weight approximately 2,000 pounds each.

The horses that pull the Main Street trolleys are fed and bathed in the morning. Around 8:00am they are loaded into a trailer and taken to the Magic Kingdom Car Barn where they are put in harness and hooked and ready to go by 9:00am.

While the trolley is heavy—when loaded with guests it can weigh about 4,000 pounds—it is so well balanced that once it gets moving, it takes only minimal effort to keep it in motion. That's one of the reasons that Disney has started to grease the track just outside the car barn to help it get started.

When Walt Disney World opened, there were four horse-drawn trolleys and it cost a dime or an "A" ticket to go one way either up or down the street. Today, only one trolley operates, and soon after the 1:00pm trolley show (that was first performed in 2002) it is pulled off the street to avoid congestion because of the parades and crowds.

The Original Artwork

Architect Michael Graves had complete creative control over every aspect of Walt Disney World's Swan and Dolphin resort hotels, from uniforms to room keys.

The murals were rendered in miniature by Graves and then the builder, Tishman Realty & Construction Company, commissioned Maer-Murphy Inc. (a company specializing in murals and decorative finishes) to follow those designs and execute the final full-sized paintings.

In a 4,000 square foot studio under the Manhattan Bridge in Brooklyn, shifts of eight artists worked on Belgium fireproof linen canvases up to 40 feet long to create 64 dramatic floral-patterned murals, which ranged in size from 200–600 square feet for the walls of the 56,000 square-foot ballroom.

The artists painted in teams, each responsible for different mural elements. The fast-paced process, using more than 160 gallons of paint for the ballroom murals alone, achieved a consistent feel throughout each series without sacrificing the individual artists' touches.

As the murals were completed, they were rolled onto carpet spools and driven to Walt Disney World. Once there, they were stretched and stapled onto large birch-wood frames, eight to twenty-three feet above the floor, and finished with trim molding.

Fifteen doors leading to audio-visual control rooms posed a special challenge. Workers cut out the canvas around these passageways, then re-stretched new canvas directly onto the doors. Artists then painted the doors on-site, integrating the pattern.

The Maer-Murphy team produced other murals that were painted on canvas at the studio and then affixed directly to the hotel's walls, such as a nine by one-hundred-and-twenty-nine foot floral patterned mural hanging behind the lobby reception desk, seven stairwell murals composed of a collage of textures and geometric patterns, and ten floral-patterned corridor murals.

One of the highlights was the Copa Banana Night Club that featured three giant fruit murals and three-dimensional fruits made of hand-painted wooden cut-outs which festoon the furniture. These works included a fifty-foot long banana bar; watermelon, cantaloupe, and grapefruit drink rails up to ten feet long; and palm tree cut-outs thirteen feet high.

Some artwork was produced on-site, such as the three-and-one-half by two-hundred-and-forty-two foot hand-painted wooden leaf valance that edged the ceiling of Harry's Safari Bar and Grille and the five-foot square checkerboard patterns painted directly onto the light blue wall covering in Tubbi Checkers Buffeteria, the 1950s-themed fast food restaurant.

In the Coral Café, twenty-four oversized fish (catfish, mousefish, and even a school of fish sporting mortar boards) seem to "float" from the ceiling, with another twenty affixed to the walls. The four-to-six foot long wooden cut-outs were by artist Robert Braun.

Braun painted the floral-patterned mural for the rotunda lobby and also created beach scene murals, complete with palm tees, beach balls, and pails and shovels to line the corridor, while the carpet design was meant to resemble a sandy beach with beach towels, balls, and suntan lotion designs.

As is common at Walt Disney World, some of these areas had back stories. Harry's Safari Bar and Grille was owned by a legendary traveler who roamed the world in search of gourmet treasure which included open-flame cooked meats, fish, and vegetables flavored with exotic herbs. The staff never knows when Harry may stop in, so his table is always ready and Harry's Safari Ale is always in the cooler.

In addition, over 4,500 prints of classic paintings hang throughout the hotel representing artists who had influenced Graves' style, including Picasso, Matisse, Hockney, and Rousseau.

Raven Totem Pole

Duane Pasco, though not a descendant of Pacific Northwest Indians, is considered one of the most adept among the handful of Canadian and American master carvers working today. He was responsible for both 55-foot tall totem poles in the lobby of the Wilderness Lodge. Pasco said:

> These totem poles measure 3-feet wide at the top and 5-feet wide at the bottom and each is constructed of two 27-foot sections spliced together. The choice of characters and their placement were the choice of Disney World's consultants.

> I made very detailed drawings for this project because there were to be three assistants helping me: Pat Huggins, Loren White, and Scott Jensen. I drew front, side, three-quarter views and lots of cross sections. In this way the client, the contractor and all the carvers can see exactly what the end product should look like.

After the poles were carved, they were finished with Thompson's Water Seal and then painted. The installation, which occurred during January 1994, took five days. The poles are flanked by stone walls and tied to steel I-beams.

The Raven Totem Pole is located in front of the Whispering Canyon Café. Both poles are read from the bottom to the top.

Beginning at the bottom of the Raven pole is the image of the Whale Chief who had a beautiful daughter, Dolphin. Mountain Lion asked to marry her but was refused and, in his anger, scratched Whale Chief's throat with his claws, leaving scratches so deep they have remained on many whales ever since.

Frog is known as the great communicator and made peace between Whale Chief and Mountain Lion. As part of that agreement, Whale Chief decided to hold an archery contest and the animal that came closest with its arrow to the mark would be allowed to wed his daughter.

Wolf, Bear, Eagle, Beaver, Otter, Kingfisher, and many others tried, but while some of their arrows came very close to the center of the mark, none of them were perfect.

Finally, the little Wren asked to try. Because he was so tiny, he had made his own bow and arrow from two spruce needles. His needlelike arrow flew straight to the center of the mark, winning the right to marry the Whale Chief's daughter.

All the other animals roared and shrieked in fury and started to chase the small Wren, who flew up to a knot hole where he was safe and where most wrens have nested ever since.

Hootis, the Bear Chief, and his wife had two small cubs who could transform themselves into humans if they so chose. They went with Wren and his new bride as their protectors when they moved to a small island.

Beautiful Dolphin would leap out of the water for joy whenever her husband sang and danced for her. However, she missed her friends, the Salmon people. Wren had Frog call the Salmon people back from their journeys to the surrounding rivers and islands.

The Salmon people did return and were so happy to see Dolphin again that they leapt up the rivers and over the waterfalls. Many new salmon were born in these waters but left to grow large and shiny, vowing they would return to the river where they had been born.

At the top of the pole is Raven, representing another version of the trickster bird flying into the Sky Chief's house where, with his beak, he cleverly untied the double cords and knots that tightly bound a painted box. Opening the lid, Raven lifted out the moon and then broke off chips from the cedar box to form stars. He flung them all into the dark night sky where they have spread their light.

Next, he reached into the box and flung out a fiery ball of sun as a gift to all the animals, birds, and humans to brighten the world.

The final tale of the raven is another variation of the story told on the large cedar totem pole outside the Trading Post in the Canada pavilion at World Showcase. This particular story is central to the Northwest Indian's spiritual beliefs about the origins of the world.

Eagle Totem Pole

Artist Duane Pasco was responsible for both towering totem poles in the lobby of the Wilderness Lodge. While they were placed on opposite sides of the lobby, following tradition, they were placed not directly across from each other.

Pasco's wife, Katie, wrote:

> The goal in designing the totem poles was to use legend and lore that was common among many tribes of the Northwest Coast but not necessarily specific to any one tribe. This was easy to accomplish because the figures and the stories they represent remain fairly consistent. Characters on the Disney poles are pan-coastal in nature, with a particular attempt to portray figures not associated with inherited stories or family crests.

Pasco and his assistants began cutting away material with chainsaws. For finer details they used adzes, knives, and other traditional carving tools. The entire process took roughly six months. The poles were made from four old-growth red cedars each about five feet in diameter at the base.

The big cedars had to be hollowed out and there was considerable rot inside that had to be removed. Pasco reinforced the centers by splicing in new wood. When he was finished, he had half-cylinders that were about four inches thick on each edge and about one foot thick in the center.

The story of the Eagle Totem Pole, located in front of the check-in counter, begins at the bottom with the Bear Chief. Frog tells the Bear Chief that he should hold a potlatch feast for his young nephew, Bear Cub. (On the pole, the Bear Cub is emerging from between the Chief's ears because traditionally, nephews were to be trained by their uncles who would educate them in the ways of the Bear Clan.)

A great painted shield of copper, the symbol of highest wealth, shows the design of Staget, the magical spirit between animals and humans. The Bear Chief plans to give this item of great value to his nephew during the potlatch feast.

Klu-kun, the Mountain Goat, sits on a pole holding the copper shield to protect it. Mountain Goat once helped a young copper seeker to climb down the mountain cliffs by lending him his hooves.

A short section with a hole is where Ksem Wed-Zin, the Mouse Woman, lives and monitors the animals and humans around her. She is famous for helping young people, intervening when she feels that a young human or animal has been hurt or abused.

Above her are the clamshells that are another tale of Raven when there were only a few animals and no humans in the world. Raven was flying over a long, narrow arm of sand that was thrust far out into the sea. He saw a large clam lying on that beach and opened it with his powerful beak.

In this way, Raven released the first humans who ever walked on earth. These humans were small, no larger than the size of the smallest finger, but as they went running toward freedom, they began to grow and grow until they reached a normal size. They built huge sea canoes and paddled along the coastlines until soon they had populated the world.

Beaver with a chew stick sits between Raven and Eagle because these two great supernatural birds have not always lived in peace together. Once, they argued over who should grab the smaller Beaver's crest and take it for his own. Beaver prevented this from happening by threatening to unleash a giant beaver larger than the two of them combined. Beaver dove into the pond and made a hole so that the water drained away revealing this monstrous beaver hiding at the bottom of the pond.

At the top of the pole is the Eagle who heard a girl crying far out to sea because she had gone away to marry one of the Undersea People but grew sad and lonely for her family and her own people. Eagle flew out and picked up the girl and started to fly her back to her family, but the girl was so curious that she didn't listen to Eagle's warning not to look down and it caused both of them to fall into the sea in front of the girl's village. They both struggled to swim ashore.

Eagle likes to help, which is why atop his head sits three small Taan-skeels. These are the watchmen for all humans and animals. Wearing tall, shading hats, Taan-skeels keep their eyes wide open day and night, peering endlessly out to sea along the beaches and deep inside the shadows of the forest to help protect the village houses.

Carolwood Pacific Room

According to the Imagineering back story, adjacent to Disney's Wilderness Lodge a team of railroad workers in the 1860s found an ideal location to set up camp as they built the transcontinental railway. They built themselves a place to stay but moved on once their job was completed.

So, even though it was built later than the Wilderness Lodge, the Villas at Disney's Wilderness Lodge was designed to look as if it "pre-dated" that resort to incorporate the story. The design is reminiscent of turn-of-the century hotels built by early railroad workers of the national parks of the American West during the Golden Age of railroad travel.

The Villas at Disney's Wilderness Lodge officially opened on November 15, 2000, becoming the fifth Disney Vacation Club location. When it opened it featured a small, quiet room off to the right side of the lobby called the Iron Spike Room. An iron spike was traditionally used on railroad ties.

In fall 2007, it was renamed the Carolwood Pacific Room thanks to the efforts of Michael Broggie, co-founder of the Carolwood Historical Society and son of Imagineer Roger Broggie, who said:

> The Iron Spike room name fit the railroad theme, but I wanted to see the name truly represent the backyard railroad that played such an important role in Disney history.

From 1950–1953, Walt Disney transported friends and family through his elaborately landscaped backyard in Holmby Hills, California, on a 1/8th scale train dubbed the Carolwood Pacific Railroad. It was named for the street where Walt lived at the time (355 North Carolwood Drive) as well as to reference the Central Pacific Railroad from the turn of the century. Walt called the engine, based on a Central Pacific 1872 locomotive, the *Lilly Belle*. Michael Broggie recalled:

I vividly remember my first ride, straddling one of those freight cars as it rocked back and forth. I remember entering a long tunnel, which was absolutely pitch black. You could hear the chuffing of the engine echoing off of this long tunnel. You could smell and taste the coal smoke. You could feel the vibration of the track. Walt had created an experience that excited every one of your senses.

From the beginning, the room was decorated with train memorabilia and framed photos related to Walt Disney's love of trains. Broggie helped the Imagineers locate the authentic artifacts that fill the room.

A cattle car, a gondola car (both hand-built by Imagineer Roger Broggie), and a stretch of track all from the actual backyard railroad was loaned to the area by Walt's oldest daughter, Diane Disney Miller and her Disney Family Foundation. The cars feature the Carolwood Pacific "Fair Weather Route" logo.

The rest of Walt's Carolwood Pacific Railroad is displayed at the Walt Disney Family Museum in San Francisco. Another car from the train is displayed at the Disney Barn at Griffith Park in Los Angeles.

A painting on display, "Walt's Magical Barn", created by artist Bob Byerley in 2001 to celebrate Walt Disney's 100th birthday was used as the cover for a book published by the Carolwood Pacific Society.

Also on display in a lucite case is a special limited-edition re-creation of the CP 173 *Lilly Belle* locomotive, tender, gondola car, and the yellow caboose from Walt's Carolwood Pacific Railroad. It was produced in 2000 in garden gauge (1:24 scale) by Hartland Locomotive Works of Indiana. This limited edition (1500 units) was offered only through Disneyland, Walt Disney World (five locations), the Disney Direct catalog, and Disney Galleries. It originally sold for $595 and came with a solid oak base and an authentic piece of rail from Walt's backyard railroad.

Olivia's Café

The first DVC resort opened on December 20, 1991, and was known just as Disney's Vacation Club Resort until January 1996 when it was renamed Disney's Old Key West Resort to distinguish it from the newer DVC properties.

The restaurant at Old Key West is Olivia's Café. According to the Imagineers, the back story of the restaurant was that Olivia Farnsworth, sixty years old (but "going on twenty"), lived in a small cottage along Turtle Krawl. She loved cooking, but did not have the money to open a restaurant of her own. She was very friendly and proud of her cooking. Almost daily she would invite curious passersby who smelled her cooking to come in to her dining room and pull up a chair to enjoy what she had prepared.

Soon, these visits became more and more frequent, both for the locals and for visiting out-of-towners. Olivia quickly ran out of room and everything else. People began bringing their own tables and chairs and even silverware and then left them there for their next visit. That's why the silverware and the chairs in the restaurant are mismatched and add to a homey, family-type atmosphere.

The Imagineers wrote:

> Soon she began doubling recipes, then double doubling. Then triple doubling, until the math got ugly. She pulled up more chairs, added more tables, and sat people on the porch, until the floor plan got all cattywhumpus. Finally, to the town's great relief, Olivia made it official, cinched up her apron ,and hung out her shingle.

The Imagineers even included "A Little Note from Miss Olivia" on the original menu along with her photo:

> The long and short of it is, I never intended to be any kind of big-time restaurant owner. I just happened to have this cozy cottage I called home and my kitchen just happened to be on the leeward side where aromas could wander out along Turtle Krawl. Seems like every time

I turned on the stove, 'specially early in the morning, folks would drop by with a friendly smile and a healthy appetite. I didn't mind. I'd just pull another chair up to the table. Then one more chair, and one more chair....

'Course, I admit I've sure had my share of helping hands from more than a few friends along the way. Miss Vickey, for instance, is my kind of people. She may not exactly fit into any proper pigeonhole, but she's been a true friend to me. In fact, I owe the whole look of Olivia's to Miss V's artistic eye for coordinated color combinations.

Then there's Captain Wahoo. He often doesn't have a nickel to his name, but his fish tales have kept me laughing through some lean times, and he's always made sure I get first choice of the bounty his boat brings home to the Flats.

There are lots of others who made Olivia's what it is—like Frenchie, who's sometimes a pest but always a pal, and Hank, and...well, I could go on, but I've a kitchen to keep up with and a passel of people to feed. So let me let you get on with your life with this closing thought— you're always welcome at Olivia's Cafe, where the food's always good and the atmosphere's always 100% Conch Flats.

The Gurgling Suitcase Bar next door has a story behind it as well. During Prohibition, people would come down to Key West to purchase illegal alcohol. They would pack it using their clothes to cushion the bottles so the bottles wouldn't break in their suitcases. Law enforcement officers soon caught on to this practice and when they stopped people, they would pick up the luggage and shake it to see if it "gurgled", indicating that there was liquid inside.

Mary Blair Pueblo Village Mural

One of the most artistic treasures at Walt Disney World is in the Contemporary Resort, created by Disney artist Mary Blair. She started work at the Disney studio in 1940 and contributed her unique color and design work to films like *The Three Caballeros* (1945), *Song of the South* (1946), *Cinderella* (1950), *Alice in Wonderland* (1951), and *Peter Pan* (1953). She was perhaps best known for her design work on the "it's a small world" attraction in Fantasyland at Disney's World Magic Kingdom.

A massive ninety-foot tall mural encircles the elevator shafts of the Contemporary, each wall telling a different part of the story of the children, animals, flora, and geology of the Grand Canyon. Blair called the mural the Pueblo Village.

In 1966, Walt gave Blair the opportunity to work for the first time with fired clays and textural color by hiring her to produce a 220-square foot ceramic mural for the Jules Stein Eye Institute at the UCLA Center for Health Services in Los Angeles.

Pleased with the result, Walt then assigned her to produce two facing murals for the renovation of Disneyland's Tomorrowland promenade that opened in 1967. They were each fifteen-and-a-half feet high and fifty-four feet long and again featured her familiar children-enjoying-the-future theme.

Her final project for Disney was the mural on the elevator shafts at the Contemporary that celebrates a Southwestern theme. The architect Welton Becket originally planned for the shafts to be encased in shiny metal, to capture a modern contemporary feeling.

Instead, Blair devised a more welcoming feel for the huge interior that was named the Grand Canyon Concourse. In 1971, restaurants and bars had names like the Grand Canyon Terrace Café, El Pueblo Room, Mesa Grande Lounge, and Outer Rim to suggest that natural wonder. In 1974, the Fiesta Fun Center debuted.

Each balcony was painted a different shade of earth tone to suggest the different layers of the canyon. It took eighteen months to design, produce, and install the final mural that "hid" the elevators.

Blair was inspired by prehistoric petroglyphs, pueblo murals, Navajo ceremonial art, and sand paintings. The colors were meant not just to suggest Native American art but earth and sky tones associated with the Grand Canyon.

Near the upper right of the mural that faces the monorail is a five-legged goat. All the other goats on the mural have four legs. In their art, the Navajo have the concept of "purposely imperfect" to indicate that nothing man makes should be perfect because doing so would be an affront to the Great Spirit.

Blair used over 18,000 individually hand-painted, fire-glazed, one-foot square ceramic tiles. High quality prints of her original design paintings for individual scenes were reproduced, framed, and hung throughout the hotel, sometimes over the beds in each room. The prints were removed when the resort underwent a renovation in the early 1990s.

There is a photo of Blair looking over the layout of the tiles that were laid out on large tables in sections at WED (Imagineering) in California. The tiles were shipped from California to Florida on special air-suspension trucks. When she saw the finished mural in Florida, she told writer Ross Care, "I walked into that giant concourse. My reaction was 'Oh, wow!'"

Blair did no further work for the Disney company because of the jealousy some Imagineers had over the favoritism shown her while Walt was alive. With the death of Roy O. Disney in 1971, she no longer had a champion to protect her or to offer any new work and the alcoholism that had long plagued her and her husband, Lee, got out of control, adding to her downward spiral.

Robert Stern's Design Concepts

New York architect Robert A. M. Stern's design philosophy is "interpretation rather than innovation", meaning that his designs reflect his affection for the past reinterpreted in his own vision.

CEO Michael Eisner called Stern a "Super Imagineer" and the two developed a strong friendship. Eisner's vacation home in Aspen was designed by Stern, who also served on The Walt Disney Company's board of directors from 1992 to 2003 and has designed many buildings for Walt Disney World, including the Casting Center, the Boardwalk Resort, and the urban design work for the city of Celebration.

"You have to remember that Disney is a dream world rooted in a dream view of life and architectural history," he said.

The initial Imagineering designs for hotels near Epcot struggled with trying to find an international theme, but plans for both a Bavarian hotel and a French hotel were rejected before Stern was brought in to the project.

Newport Bay Club in Disneyland Paris is drawn from Stern's original designs for the Yacht and Beach Club resorts. It was to be one huge hotel over a mile in length, the same distance as walking from the Mexico Pavilion to the Canada Pavilion on the promenade of the World Showcase.

It was decided that one huge hotel so close to the massive Swan and Dolphin resorts would be too overwhelming at the time. So Stern redesigned his concept into one continuous structure with two related themes: New England and mid-Atlantic shore. That is why there are evergreens rather than palm trees to landscape the areas.

The Yacht and Beach Club resorts were meant to invoke the more genteel turn-of-the-century civility and charm.

The Yacht Club is more formal, nautical, and reminiscent of the rustic yet elegant, shingle-covered Victorian seaside resorts that were built toward the end of the 19th century in New England towns such as Newport, Marblehead, Cape Cod, and Bar Harbor. It was meant to be more sophisticated and sedate, so gray colors were used.

Shingle-style homes were never the more humble dwellings of the local fishermen. They were meant to be vacation "cottages" for the very wealthy. As the new look became popular, Shingle-style homes popped up in fashionable neighborhoods far from the seashore. Eventually, the style fell out of favor in the early 1900s but experienced a revival in the second half of the 20th century.

The Beach Club is more informal and airy in expression. It is modeled on the many Stick-style cottages and resorts that could be found in towns like Cape May, New Jersey. Stern used blue and white to capture what he called the "sand between your toes" feeling.

Stick-style buildings are noted for a number of unique features all united by the use of "sticks" or flat-board banding and other applied ornamentation in geometric patterns that adorn the exterior clapboard wall surface. High compression fiberboard called Werzalit was used at the resort to simulate the traditional beaded clapboard siding of shore hotels.

Stormalong Bay is a three-acre water mini-park encompassing 750,000 gallons of water and featuring waterfalls, a lazy circular river, pulsating water jets, one of the highest Disney resort waterslides (disguised as a pirate shipwreck), and an elevated tanning deck. However, perhaps the most unique aspect of the pool area is the sandy bottom. The lighthouse at the end of the dock is meant to be reminiscent of a lighthouse in Cape May originally built in 1859.

A large number of non-resort guests were taking advantage of the area, so in 1997 a white fence with only three entrances was built to surround the pool, with cast members checking IDs of people wanting to use it.

PART THREE

The Rest of Walt Disney World

While many people think of Walt Disney World just in terms of its four theme parks, the property contains many other interesting opportunities. A commitment to sports and fitness was always part of the original plan for WDW from 1971.

ESPN Wide World of Sports Complex, a 220-acre state of the art sports facility, opened in March 1997 and was re-branded as part of the ESPN franchise in February 2010. It hosts more than a hundred athletic related events a year.

The facility features multiple competition venues, including 16 baseball/softball fields, plus the almost 10,000 seat Champion Stadium, 18 multi-purpose outdoor fields for soccer, football, and lacrosse, two field houses for basketball, volleyball, and other indoor sports, the New Balance Track & Field facility and cross-country course, and a tennis court complex with 10 courts.

In September 2002, the Disney company reached an out-of-court settlement for an undisclosed amount of money with two businessmen.

Many years earlier, in 1987, Palm Harbor, Florida-based All Pro Sports Camps founders Edward Russell and Nicholas Stracick met with Disney executives to pitch a sports complex they called Sports Island to be built at Walt Disney World.

They showed Disney a model and gave them a business plan. Disney rejected the idea but within a few years crafted the sports facility known as Disney's Wide World of Sports. In August 2000, a jury returned a verdict for the plaintiffs with damages in the amount of $240 million, a fraction of the $1.5 billion originally sought by the businessmen.

Louis M. Meisinger, Disney's executive vice president and general counsel, said:

> The evidence was overwhelming that the idea for the sports complex was independently created by Walt Disney employees. We feel that this verdict was driven by [an] appeal to the jury's prejudices against corporations and business in general.

Most of the moderate and deluxe hotels, as well as the Disney Vacation Club resorts, offer health clubs, fitness centers, and spas to guests and visitors.

The Contemporary, Polynesian, and Old Key West resorts offer basic gyms. The Yacht and Beach Clubs, BoardWalk, Wilderness Lodge, Coronado Springs, and the Animal Kingdom Lodge offer health clubs with limited additional services, such as massage and saunas.

The Grand Floridian and Saratoga Springs offer complete and expensive spa services in addition to the regular fitness equipment.

Among the more elaborate health clubs are the Ship Shape Health Club at Yacht and Beach, Muscles and Bustles Health Club at the Boardwalk Inn, Sturdy Branches Health Club at Wilderness Lodge, La Vida Health Club at Coronado Springs, and the Zahanati Massage and Fitness Center at Animal Kingdom Lodge.

The health clubs are staffed during the day, but Disney resort guests can use their room keycard to access the equipment during the night. Guests of resorts with dedicated gyms have free 24-hour access to the equipment. For guests not staying at that resort, there is the option to use the area for a fee. Day passes are available, as well as length-of-stay passes.

Most of the health clubs at Walt Disney World offer treadmills, elliptical trainers, stair climbers, and weight machines for upper- and lower-body workouts. All of the fitness centers provide towels.

Since January 16, 2013, the spas, salons and fitness clubs at Walt Disney World are operated by Disney itself. They were previously operated by Niki Bryan, Inc.

While not technically a Disney hotel, the Swan and Dolphin on Disney World property also offers a health club and spa services. In addition, guests can enjoy cruises, tours, dessert parties, fishing, horseback riding, golfing, and other activities at WDW.

This section shares some of the stories about WDW areas outside the theme parks.

Original Proposal

The first tenants of the city of Celebration, Florida, took up residence in June 1996. However, to get approval for that use, years earlier Disney had to share its plans for the area south of U.S. Highway 192.

In May 1991, Disney presented its initial proposal for Celebration to the East Central Florida Regional Planning Council for review.

Space for 20,000 residents and 15,000 employees would include 8,000 "moderately upscale" homes of all sizes and values that would be built in four themed villages between 1993 and 2015. Three of the villages would wrap around championship golf courses.

All homes would include a fiber-optic computer network to allow homeowners to select a movie without going to a video store. Shoppers would be able to call up a recipe and get a printout of ingredients, including their location in the grocery store. The system would connect with the hospital so that residents could talk directly to a doctor and have things like their blood pressure monitored. The plans included:

Celebration Center: A two-million square foot international shopping district with famous name retailers from many nations that was projected to attract ten million visitors a year. It would be designed by architect Helmut Jahn of Chicago with the first million square feet scheduled for an early 1995 opening.

Enterprise Park: A 240,000 square foot office center designed by Italian architect Aldo Rossi. The first phase was a three million square foot office park.

Residential Community: Four villages with a variety of architectural styles. It would include 8,000 units in a pedestrian-oriented setting, twenty miles of walk and bikeways, a unique video library with a fiber-optic link to homes, plus an electronically indexed grocery store.

The Disney Institute: "A new kind of Disney learning resort to entertain, educate and revitalize guests with movies, gourmet cooking and lectures including an Entertainment Arts Academy, performing arts center and fitness spa, master-planned by AIA Gold Medal architect Charles Moore". CEO Michael Eisner had been promoting the concept since 1984 which he described as the "cultural heart and soul of the community".

Medical and Health Center: Wellness services and a 150-bed medical facility.

Environmental Center: An adjoining expansive wilderness area to teach residents and guests about the heritage of Florida wildlife and forest lands.

Three Championship Golf Courses: Winding through Celebration villages, the courses include a signature hole course where designers' kiosks will provide video on each hole's design and tips for playing it.

Schools/Civic Areas: Schools are being planned to cater to the needs of residents, with innovative techniques and guest-teacher plan in structures which might be designed by world-famous architects whose talents will be applied for the first time toward classroom design. Other civic amenities were planned as well

The Workplace: Visitors will be able to enjoy the creative ingenuity of industrial "wizards" from around the world designing and making everything from tennis balls to compact discs in facilities created to inform and entertain. Designed to promote the free enterprise system and industrial wizardry, tourists would pay to watch a product's creation.

Multimodal Station: A transportation facility to respond to the needs of the region and able to accommodate all forms of rail and other ground transit systems.

According to the proposal, upon completion of the Development of Regional Impact Study review process, the property would be de-annexed from Reedy Creek Improvement District and fall under the jurisdiction of Oseola County. Even after the actual de-annexation, Disney still retained ownership of some assets like the downtown area and the golf course, but they were both later sold.

The Early Years

Celebration, Florida, is a planned community that was created by the Walt Disney Company in 1994 on Disney-owned land. For nearly two decades, the area remained undeveloped and was sometimes used as a place to relocate alligators found in nearby Walt Disney World.

Initially, the city of Celebration covered approximately 4,900 acres with an additional 4,700 acres of wetland left in pristine condition. Originally, it was run by the Celebration Company, a fully owned subsidiary of the Disney Company, rather than by elected officials.

Its general purpose was to create a romanticized modern version of a small town with homes clustered around a pedestrian-friendly central business area featuring restaurants, shops, offices, and a movie theater.

Disney enlisted many famous architects to design the buildings, and while it was not specifically intended to suggest the storybook small-town atmosphere usually associated with some Disney projects, the city does invoke what many believe is a Disney-esque "feel". The architects included Michael Graves, Philip Johnson, Charles Moore (and his partner Arthur Andersson), Caesar Pelli, William Rawn, Robert Venturi, and Denise Scott-Brown.

The overall "master plan" was the work of architects Robert A.M. Sterrn and Jacquelin Robertson, who also designed the commercial and residential buildings downtown.

Stern stated in 1996 that the idea behind Celebration was:

> To recapture the idea of a traditional town, traditional in spirit but modern in terms of what we know about how people live.

Stern and Robertson were influenced by towns as geographically disparate as East Hampton, New York, and Charleston, South Carolina. The houses in Celebration are representative of a number of regional prototypes—in particular, Classical, Victorian, Colonial Revival, Coastal, Mediterranean, and French. Ray Gindroz of the

Pittsburgh UDA Architects created a "pattern book" using these prototypes that was meant to ensure "both diversity and harmony in the architecture".

According to a 1996 guidebook to Celebration:

> Celebration is designed to offer a return to a more sociable and civic-minded way of life. It is a walking town. The town plan places special emphasis on restoring streets and sidewalks to the public realm on the assumption that streets should belong to people, not cars.... All the residential areas in Celebration Village are within reach of one another and of Downtown Celebration, which means that everyone will be able to walk to school or to the movies.

The Italian architect, Aldo Rossi, was the designer of Celebration Place, the office buildings north of the downtown area near U.S. Route 192, where Disney Cruise Lines, Yellow Shoes Marketing, Disney Institute, and other Disney divisions have maintained office space for over a decade.

On November 18, 1995, a lottery was held for the opportunity to buy one of the first 351 home lots. Those lots were sold quickly, and a six-month waiting list was established for the next openings. However, rushing to complete those early homes resulted in some less-than-perfect construction that later caused problems.

Many things that were initially announced did not occur, including that the houses would be connected to Celebration Hospital through fiber optic cables accessible by home computers that would put residents in direct contact with a doctor.

Other proposed elements that never appeared included the Disney Institute campus and the enivronmental education center adjoining the expansive wilderness area that would teach residents and guests about the heritage of Florida wildlife and forest lands. A performing arts center and a fitness spa had also been in the plans.

Disney de-annexed the property from the Reedy Creek Improvement District in 2004 to Lexin Capital, a private real estate investment company. The current population is approximately 8,502 people.

The Story Behind the Story

Downtown Disney, which was three separate unconnected sections in terms of an overall story, has been re-imagined as a cohesive retail and entertainment venue, encompassing 120 acres, called Disney Springs.

Florida has one of the largest concentrations of freshwater springs on Earth—more than 900 of them. A few springs gave birth to towns, including Silver Springs in Marion County, Green Cove Spring in Clay County, and De Leon Springs in Volusia County.

The Imagineering storyline is that Disney Springs also attracted its first settlers "more than a century ago" and, over the decades, the town continued to expand naturally into four distinct districts: Town Center, The Landing, Marketplace, and West Side.

The architecture of Disney Springs varies by district, with the West Side featuring elements like the remains of an elevated train track from the fictional 1950 Golden Centennial Expo.

Imagineer Theron Skees said:

> The story is really of a small town that grew up around a natural spring. It's a story that's really not unlike lots of small towns in Florida that grew up in the same kind of way. It has sort of a nod to the history of Florida as it developed and grew up over the years.

Imagineer Briana Ricci, in charge of character paint and finishing, said about creating the actual springs:

> We started with a base coat, followed by air compressor hoppers that poured out our accent colors which resulted in a color blend you would get in a nice water color painting. We only had a half hour or so before the cement dried completely and became as solid as a rock which made it all a challenge.

> We included colored glass, which was a very critical element because we have a limited palette, so we needed something to enhance and push our colors and depth, something bright and vibrant as well as long lasting with zero maintenance.

Natural elements that already existed in the area such as oak trees, cypress trees, and plants were saved and incorporated into the design. However, Imagineering also created some other elements like carving exposed tree roots by the water so that the entire area felt integrated.

Disney Springs was inspired in part by Kismet, Florida, now a vanished town that was once located in the Ocala National Forest area. Before the early 1900s, it was a new community built around citrus groves near Alexander Springs. Kismet was where Walt and Roy Disney's parents met and married, although they moved to Chicago not long afterward where Walt and Roy were born.

Skees stated:

> When Walt came to Florida and bought the property to begin with, we love the idea that maybe his parents told him about the area and when it was purchased that this idea of Disney Springs was sort of central to it.

The goal of the Imagineers was to capture the warmth and nostalgia of an old-fashioned small town neighborhood, in much the same spirit as Main Street USA, from a simpler time but with an "upscale vibe" when it came to the stores and restaurants. They didn't want just another shopping and dining location, but for guests to be immersed in an experience.

Tom Staggs, Disney Chief Operating Officer and the former chair of Walt Disney Parks and Resorts, stated:

> That sense of welcome, that sense of embrace, especially with this great center around the Springs, is going to be instinctive and natural for our guests.

> We get asked ... why we spend so much time on the storytelling, even in a place that isn't a theme park. It guides our development and keeps us rooted in a sense of place.

Jock Lindsey's Hangar Bar

Disney's purchase in 2012 of the entire Lucasfilm catalog for four billion dollars included the beloved Indiana Jones franchise. Their first use of that acquisition was the creation of Jock Lindsey's Hangar Bar in Disney Springs.

Jock Lindsey was a minor character in the movie *Raiders of the Lost Ark* (1981) portrayed by actor Fred Sorenson who rescued Indy from the Peruvian Hovito natives with his seaplane. The character was an American freelance pilot whose background was as a stunt pilot performing in Midwest airshows.

After a flight-related tragedy, he relocated to Venezuela where he was often hired to fly archeologist Indiana Jones to remote locations. According to the original screenplay, he was supposed to be British. His pet was a Burmese python snake named "Reggie".

According to the newly created Disney legend, Lindsey took Jones over Florida in 1938 to help hunt down the location of the fabled Fountain of Youth. Lindsey spotted a small town that he liked and returned in 1948 to establish an airplane hangar, air tower, and runway on its waterfront and operate an air tour service.

His fellows members of the Society of Explorers and Adventurers (SEA) would drop by for an occasional drink and in 1955, the area was officially established as a hangar bar and was littered with artifacts and memoribilia from their adventures.

The concrete bar top is made to look as if it was once used as a work bench. Ceiling fans are made out of plane propellers, and walls are adorned with vintage travel posters and postcards and letters between Indy, Jock, and other characters.

Imagineer Theron Skees said:

> He only had about a minute of air time in the original movie, and it was fun expanding on that. We were coming at it from the aspect that Jock is a pilot first and an adventurer's guide second.

In addition to references to the first three theatrical *Indiana Jones* movies, Jock Lindsey's Hangar Bar also alludes to elements from the "expanded adventures" such as *The Young Indiana Jones Chronicles* and *Indiana Jones and the Fate of Atlantis*, and Jock Lindsey's roles in *Indiana Jones and the Tomb of the Gods* and *The Further Adventures of Indiana Jones* story "The Sea Butchers".

The bar also contains nods to other Disney properties including *Star Wars*, *The Rocketeer*, and *Iron Man*, as well as references to famous aviators such as Amelia Earhart and Charles Lindbergh.

The bar's address at 1138 Seaten Avenue references a George Lucas feature film tradition to include the number from his first theatrical film *THX 1138* (1971). In addition:

- From *Raiders* comes the golden fertility idol at the top of the bar's bookcase. The head piece for the staff of Ra is in the lost-and-found bin located near the bathrooms

- From *The Temple of Doom* comes voodoo dolls of Indy, Short Round, and Willie Scott, positioned on a shelf. Also from that film is a coaster from Club Obi Wan in Shanghai, China. The cool-headed monkey drink and souvenir mug reference the monkey brain-eating sequence in the film.

- From *The Last Crusade* comes the image of the grail cup on a sign stating "artifacts no longer taken as payment".

There are several references to Reggie, including an empty cage, a signature drink with a snake swizzle stick, and an outside dry-docked steamboat named after the pet reptile.

All of the menu items have names that cleverly reference the films, including Rolling Boulder Sliders, Tanis Tacos, Lao Che's Revenge, Dr. Elsa's She-deviled Eggs, Hovito Mojito, Poisonless Dart, and Brody's Brats.

Jock and Indy may be long gone, but this location honors their memories and immerses guests in their legendary adventures.

The World of Disney Store

When the World of Disney store opened October 2, 1996, at Downtown Disney, its first guests were given a colorful character map to help orient themselves to the massive 51,000 square feet of retail space referred to as "The Largest Disney Character Shop in the World".

As Walt Disney World publicity described the World of Disney Store when it first opened:

> It's paradise for everyone, from the newest Mickey fan to the avid Disneyana enthusiast. Disney merchandise is arranged so artfully that this remarkable store is an attraction itself. As you enter, you'll pass beneath giant airships and into lands of endless fascination.
>
> The journey starts in The Great Hall and 60-foot high Rotunda, where eight more fantasy airships averaging 20 feet in length are piloted by numerous Disney characters. State-of-the-art, high fidelity sound comparable only to a movie theater adds to your delight.

When the World of Disney Store opened, each room was given a colorful name to help guests more easily locate a particular item and guests were encouraged to "bring home the magic!" The rooms were:

- Enchanted Dining Room (candy, gourmet foods, housewares).
- Exotic Animals Room, to the right of the Enchanted Dining Room (men's clothing, ties, boxers, hosiery). In 2006, as part of the store's 10th anniversary celebration, this room was re-themed to the Pirates of the Caribbean and Stitch and renamed the Adventure Room. Pirates in a jail cell and another outside at a steering wheel were allusions to the original theme park ride.
- The Magic Room, to the left of the Enchanted Dining Room (adult sleepwear, slippers, boxers).
- The Great Hall and Rotunda, a long hallway straight ahead from the Enchanted Dining Room (popular souvenirs, adult apparel, headwear, luggage, backpacks, sunglasses).

- The Map Room, straight ahead down the hallway (Disney souvenirs, stationery, decorative figurines, photo albums, personalization).
- The Bird Room, to the right of the Map Room (women's apparel collections, latest women's fashions).
- The Villains Room, to the left of the Map Room (Disney watches, jewelry, clocks, decorative gifts).
- The Carnival Room, straight ahead from the Map Room (princess costumes, kids' sleepwear, dolls, kids' bath and body).
- The Snow White Room, to the right of the Carnival Room (infant and toddler apparel, kid's bedding, baby books, baby plush toys).
- The Wonderland Room, straight ahead from the Carnival Room, (kids' souvenirs, children's apparel, media and books, plush toys). In 2006, this room was renamed the Princess Room and was redesigned to look like a great hall in a fairy-tale castle. With the opening of the Bibbidi Bobbidi Boutique in 2006, books and media were relocated to the Map Room. Supposedly, the "owner" of the boutique is the Fairy Godmother from *Cinderella*.

With the opening of Disney Springs, the interior of The World of Disney was reconfigured again, although many of the original decorative elements remain.

The concept of a store "with the largest selection of Disney character merchandise in the world" was so appealing that a second, slightly smaller version of The World of Disney store opened in 2001 in the Downtown Disney shopping district at the Disneyland Resort in California.

A third site opened October 2004 inside a three-story New York building that formerly housed the traditional Disney Store. It closed in late December 2009.

On July 12, 2012, another World of Disney Store opened at Disney Village in Disneyland Paris as part of a refurbishment of that area, making it the third World of Disney store in current operation.

WDW Team Disney Building

Disney CEO Michael Eisner decided to build another Team Disney building near Walt Disney World to consolidate many of the company's leased offices spread around the Orlando metropolitan region.

Eisner was impressed with the work that Japanese architect Arata Isozaki had done for the Museum of Contemporary Art (MOCA) in Los Angeles that had opened in 1986.

The July 1992 issue of *Smithsonian* magazine stated:

> Isozaki returned with a scheme he likened to an ocean liner—a sleek, extended, four-story office with a huge funnel amidships, reflected in a pool. Around the funnel is an asymmetrical cluster of brightly colored cubes. The collision of skylights, entrance lobby and related spaces creates a tremendous sense of expectation as one approaches the building.

The central sundial is built out of Dryvet, a form of styrofoam. If it had been built out of concrete, there would have been a structural problem with support.

The cone rises 120 feet in the air. Isozaki intended that a person inside would feel "lost in time" in an experience that would feel "timeless". It was not meant just to be an ornamental amusement.

The interior features a series of eighty-eight granite stepping stones inscribed with famous quotations all chosen by Michael Eisner himself who sat up many nights surrounded by books of quotations, poetry, and proverbs. The Tennessee river rock surrounding the stones is a traditional type of material used in Japanese shrines.

The building was built to true north so that the sundial would be accurate. The building's roughly 900-foot length approximates the distance sound travels in one second and is three times larger than the Team Disney building in Anaheim.

The north and south wings of the building are rectangular, indistinctive, and quiet, and were meant to reflect the stillness of the water of the outside pool that has now been replaced with landscaping. These wings were meant to be a neutral area without distraction.

The center entrance is a chaotic mix of shapes and colors meant to be representative of the outside "real" world from which workers would transition into a calmness that would help them to focus on their jobs. When they leave, the entrance helps them to readjust to the noise and confusion of reality.

One of Isozaki's trademarks is the collision of geometrical shapes to create a sense of conflict and awareness.

Since the building houses such departments as Finance, Accounting, Business Insight & Improvement, Legal, Diversity, and Community Relations, it was felt that a calm, centered environment would help steady the workers during the tumultuous nature of their daily business activity.

Isozaki included three Japanese torii in his exterior design. Traditionally, a torii, or "gate", is found at the entrance of a Japanese Shinto shrine and is designed to cleanse the heart, soul, and mind of a person from the profane to the sacred as he proceeds into the building.

The outer of these gates is called *ichi no torii*, the second is the *ni no torii*, and the third (closest to the sanctuary) is the *san no torii*. Visitors to the Team Disney Building pass under the first two torii as they enter the parking lot and the final one as they enter the building.

Of course, since this is Disney and Isozaki had a sense of humor, the torii are in the famous silhouette of Mickey Mouse's ears.

The building opened in 1991 and was among ten projects world-wide that received the American Institute of Architects' 1992 Honor Awards because this "lively, eccentric headquarters celebrates fantasy while at the same time providing a serious, functional environment".

STOLport

While driving toward the Magic Kingdom, guests often wonder about a paved area off the right side of the road that has sometimes been used for overflow parking, for training bus drivers, for temporary storage of a variety of items, and for the staging of the tracks of the Magic Kingdom's Seven Dwarfs Mine Train attraction.

That area was actually an operating airfield known as STOLport (Short Take Off and Landing) for smaller propeller planes. The first official United States STOLport was the one at Walt Disney World that opened on October 17, 1971, on that unique area to the side of the road. The dedication ceremony was at a luncheon on October 22, 1971.

Shawnee Airlines operated scheduled passenger service between the Lake Buena Vista STOLport (sometimes referred to as the Walt Disney World Airport or by the designation "DWS", Disney World STOLport, in its earliest days) and Orlando McCoy Jetport (it did not become Orlando International Airport until 1976) as well as the Tampa International Airport. For these short hops, Shawnee used nineteen deHavilland Canada DHC-6 Twin Otter turbo-prop planes.

Shawnee's intrastate flights to fourteen Florida cities were so popular that major airlines eventually moved into key Shawnee markets, prompting a shutdown of Shawnee on December 28, 1972. As a result, commercial service to STOLport was discontinued as well and never resumed because it was considered a failed experiment.

Executive Airlines and Volusia Aviation Service also used the STOLport in a limited fashion for the first few months through January 1972 and then stopped operation. WDW's STOLport was also used by a handful of celebrities, politicians, and Disney executives.

From a 1972 advertisement:

> Shawnee Airlines ... your magic carpet into Walt Disney World.
>
> Now Shawnee has nine daily shuttle flights from McCoy Jetport, Orlando, to the Vacation Kingdom of the World. When you deplane

from your STOL flight, you are within three minutes of the Walt Disney World hotels, Magic Kingdom theme park, and the Golf Resort. Only $7.00 per person—for more information, ask your travel agent or Eastern Airlines representative.

The reason Shawnee told prospective customers to contact Eastern Airlines was because that carrier was the official airline of Walt Disney World and so tourists landing at the McCoy Jetport on an Eastern Airlines flight could make an almost instant connection for the hop to STOLport, and vice versa.

Eastern Airlines sponsored the free attraction at WDW's Tomorrowland If You Had Wings which was a two-person Omnimover ride that took guests to locations serviced by the carrier.

WDW's STOLport was meant to be the beginning of an interstate STOL transportation system. While a handful of other STOLports were opened in the U.S. in the early 1970s, they were usually for private use or testing only. The craze for STOLports was short-lived and for the most part ceased to exist by the end of the 20th century.

As one of the reasons for its demise, the airfield had few facilities like hangars to protect planes from the Florida weather. At most, the airport could handle only four aircraft at a time, although it never had that many planes operating there.

Construction of the monorail extension in 1980 to Epcot made using STOLport even more difficult for pilots. The airport was still listed as a private airfield by the FAA through the end of the 1990s but ceased being listed as such by 2004.

Over the years, a handful of buildings were added in the area, including two with the image of Sorcerer Mickey on them meaning that they are temporary field offices for Imagineers who are supervising some new construction or development nearby.

Walt Disney World Topiaries

When the Magic Kingdom opened in October 1971, one of the biggest challenges was getting the unexpected flood of guests from the parking lot to the park itself. In addition to other forms of transport, half the parking lot trams were also used to haul guests from the Ticket and Transportation Center, passing the Contemporary Resort hotel along the way, to the park entrance.

Walt Disney Imagineering (not Horticulture) was asked to quickly create a topiary garden strung out along the pathway to entertain guests on their journey.

Of course, there wasn't time to grow new topiaries that might take years to fill out, so Imagineer Tony Baxter came up with faux topiaries. He cut and burned some real foliage and then painted it so that it resembled a real plant.

Mary Poppins holding her parasol high as if she were ready to fly away, a train of elephants holding each others' tails by their trunks as they seemed to be marching slowly toward the Magic Kingdom, a giraffe casually munching on the leaves of a nearby real tree and other creations were quickly installed with plastic leaves enhancing the figures.

There was a cluster of these figures near the tram terminal area located approximately where the buses load and unload today at the front of the Magic Kingdom. A handful continued to survive but gradually disappeared until by 2003 only two acrobatic elephants outside the Magic Kingdom remained. The last remaining topiary, one of those elephants, quietly disappeared in 2011.

WDW's first real topiaries, similar to those at Disneyland, were merely representations or simple silhouette outlines of the characters or generic animal figures without any detailed features.

However, by the mid-1990s, more accessories and a splash of color were added, beginning with topiaries to promote *The Lion King* (1994) animated feature at the first Epcot International Flower and Garden Festival, to make more distinctive features and expressions. For instance, the villain Scar's actual scar became more clearly visible.

The addition of so much color was inspired by the floral floats in the Pasadena Rose Parade where Disney horticulturists could see how a variety of natural materials could be woven into a figure to provide something more distinctive and suggestive. Today, some of that natural color is enhanced by paint as well.

Disney landscape artist Bill Evans told me:

> At Disneyland we didn't have time for the traditional procedure, so we devised other methods of topiary gardening. Oversimplified, these amounted to lifting old plants out of the ground, confining their roots to containers and persuading them to assume shapes they hadn't planned on.

However, by the time of the opening of Epcot in 1982, there was the necessity for even more speed and flexibility which resulted in the use of heavy steel frames for character topiaries.

The steel frames are wrapped with chicken wire and then stuffed with unmilled sphagnum moss. Small plants or "plugs" are then planted into the sphagnum and require daily watering. Because the plants in these sphagnum figures are planted into the frame itself, they do not require any type of container—just a metal stand to keep them upright.

Each topiary has its own irrigation system due to the differing needs of various parts. For example, the arms and other extremities dry out quickly, while the bodies would rot if they were watered too much. The amount of water for each area is controlled with a system of hoses with holes for each living sculpture

Consequently, they are easily moved from one location to another and are adaptable for use as stage decorations or for special occasions.

The topiaries did not take months or years to create like the ones that first appeared at Disneyland in 1963 but just a few weeks. In addition, the frames could be cleaned out and re-used.

Guests seem to enjoy these much more colorful but temporary offspring that decorate all the WDW parks today.

Oak Trail Golf

Former Disney President and Board Chairman Card Walker was an avid golfer. In 1980, he spearheaded the construction of a six-hole golf course at Walt Disney World called Wee Links. It was built in conjunction with the PGA Tour that year and was specifically designed to introduce young people to the joys of golf as well as being an opportunity for families and beginners to enjoy the game.

In addition, Walt Disney World and the PGA created the Card Walker Award in 1981 that was presented annually to a person or group who made significant contributions to junior golf.

Walker championed junior golf from the opening of Walt Disney World in 1971. During the 1970s and 1980s, WDW hosted the International Pee Wee Championships that featured young people who later went on to become PGA and LPGA Tour players. WDW also hosted several junior golf tournaments, including the PGA Junior Championships and the Florida State High School finals.

In 1992, week-long Earth Shuttle Junior Golf Instruction Schools were held at WDW. At the time, Lake Buena Vista's head professional Rina Ritson, one of the world's foremost teachers of juniors, stated:

> So many children don't get the opportunity to play unless they're exposed to golf. But Walt Disney World offers so many really fun avenues of exposure.

Walt Disney World kicked off a 20th anniversary celebration in October 1991, marketing 20 new reasons to visit the resort based on new offerings that had recently opened. One of those reasons was that Wee Links grew from six to nine holes and was renamed Disney's Oak Trail Golf Course.

Oak Trail is a nine-hole walking course that provided a smaller venue for beginners, families, and children. For advanced players who wanted a quick warm-up, or someone who just had time for only nine holes, it was also a welcome option.

Designed by Ron Garl, and operated by Arnold Palmer Golf Management since 2011, the par-36 golf course measures 2,913 yards from the back tees. Oak Trail's holes range from 132–517 yards, with undulating target greens. The course is certified by Audubon International as a cooperative wildlife sanctuary and is located across from Disney's Grand Floridian Resort.

Golf carts are not allowed, so it is a walking course only. Throughout the year, golf lessons from beginner through expert are offered and juniors are encouraged to attend at a lower rate. WDW also offers summer week-long junior golf camps.

The Oak Trail course is meant to be enjoyed slowly with wooden benches at every hole, water fountains, and occasional gazebos. The area is filled with much natural wildlife, including turkey, deer, and waterfowl, as well as a picturesque pond.

Walt Disney World features three eighteen-hole golf courses: Palm, Magnolia, and Lake Buena Vista (a fourth, Osprey Ridge, closed on August 15, 2013). Unlike Oak Trail, each course features a particular challenge like water, sand, and narrow fairways. These courses were part of the PGA Tour from 1971–2012.

Disney lost its title sponsor when the Children's Miracle Network Hospitals did not renew, and Disney did not aggressively pursue a replacement. "We've had a wonderful 40-year relationship with the tour," stated Disney tournament spokesman Tony Morreale.

Snow White House in Florida

Some Disney treasures are not on Disney property. Here is a secret that is not found in any Disney travel guide.

In the deep forest of eastern Volusia County alongside the dark waters of Spruce Creek is a charming cottage of fantasy architecture known as the Snow White House that is virtually unknown to Disney fans. It is located off Taylor Road, roughly two miles west of I-95.

The tiny cypress-and-pine home is furnished with a miniature stairway that leads to a mock dwarfs' bedroom marked by seven little headboards. Bookshelves set atop cypress knees and gnarled wood handles adorn the Gothic wood doors.

Surrounding the house are fantasy features such as a witch's hut, dwarfs' mine shaft, and wishing well, connected by fieldstone paths.

All of this, of course, was inspired by *Snow White and the Seven Dwarfs* (1937),the milestone animated feature film that captured the hearts and imagination of many people when it was first released.

Judge Alfred K. Nippert began building the Snow White House as a playhouse in 1938 for his nieces on the 150-acre hunting and fishing retreat that he had inherited five years earlier from his father-in-law, James N. Gamble, the Ivory soap king who lived in Daytona Beach.

The Gamble estate includes acres of forest, a cracker-style lodge, a citrus packing house, azalea garden, and trails through a hardwood swamp. It was donated in 1983 to the Nature Conservancy as an historical and environmental preserve open to the public for tours. The Daytona Beach Museum manages the Gamble place for the conservancy with financial help from the Junior League of Daytona Beach.

Like so many others, the young nieces loved the Disney animated film and Nippert got carried away once the project started.

Nippert hired local carpenter Ernie Whidmeir, who prepared himself for the task by studying twenty animation cels from the film obtained from the Disney studio and by repeatedly viewing the movie.

Because of Nippert's social connections, supposedly including a friendship with Walt Disney himself, he was able to obtain the celluloids for the carpenter to use as an architectural guide and create workable blueprints. A nearly full-scale replica was completed with heavy Gothic doors featuring huge authentic strap hinges and an enormous fireplace.

The cottage was completed in March 1938. Nippert invited Walt Disney to visit—and reportedly, he did. Walt was so pleased and amazed at the detailed work that captured the fairy-tale quaintness of the film that upon his return to California, he gifted Nippert with eight life-sized dolls of Snow White and each of the Seven Dwarfs.

Snow White was displayed in the parlor in a glass coffin that Nippert had built to look like the crystal tomb in the movie. The seven Dwarf dolls were put in various corners of the room to keep a watchful eye on the sleeping little princess as they awaited the arrival of the prince and true love's kiss.

The dolls disappeared some time between the time the Nippert family closed the estate in the 1940s and the Nature Conservancy took it over in the early 1980s.

During a restoration in the early 1990s, Dana Ste. Claire and his wife, Carol, lived in the Snow White House for two years, working in their free time to restore the landmark and have furnished it with their own antiques. After they finished, they moved out.

"We're going to try to get the Disney folks interested in this ... they might come over and do a little film about the house," Dana Ste. Claire said at the time, but that never happened and this little gem has been hidden from Disney fans for many years

Except for special events open to the public, tours of Gamble Place are arranged by appointment only through the Daytona Beach Museum of Arts and Sciences.

PART FOUR

The Rest of the Story

In the first issue of the cast member newsletter *Eyes and Ears of Walt Disney World, the Vacation Kingdom of the World* (with a little pennant saying "Florida" waving above the word "Disney"), dated October 1971, this statement from Chairman of the Board Roy O. Disney appeared on the first page:

> On the eve of Walt Disney World's opening day, may I thank all of you for your spirit, your cooperation and the fine job all of you have done in getting ready for our opening. Years of planning and long hours of work have brought about this historic moment. It will be an experience none of us will forget.... You, the cast, are responsible for making Walt's dream come true ... yesterday, today and tomorrow.

One week after Walt Disney died, his older brother Roy O. Disney spoke to a group of Disney company executives and creative staff in a projection room at the Disney studio in Burbank, California. He announced that he was going to postpone his retirement:

> We are going to finish this park [in Florida], and we're going to do it just the way Walt wanted it. Don't you ever forget it. I want every one of you to do just exactly what you were going to do when Walt was alive.

While the Magic Kingdom opened at 10:00am on October 1, 1971, the official dedication of the park and Walt Disney World did not take place until a three-day weekend event held October 23–25, 1971. More than 40,000 guests were there to celebrate that historic moment. Admission was $3.50 and parking was fifty cents for the entire day. There were individual tickets for the different attractions.

At the dedication, Walt's older brother Roy O. Disney was asked by reporters why a grandfather had felt the obligation to tackle this impossible project at this point in his life. He told them:

I didn't want to have to explain to Walt when I saw him again why the dream didn't come true.

Later, Roy spent time in a boat on the Seven Seas Lagoon in front of the Magic Kingdom and when asked why he wasn't in the park to handle all the media attention, he said:

Today is my brother's day. I want them to remember my brother today.

Reporter Charlie Wadsworth wrote in an article for the December 22, 1971, edition of the *Orlando Sentinel*:

It was Roy Disney's guidance and leadership that brought Walt Disney World to its opening. He was completely dedicated to building the dreams of his brother Walt. They say a little of Roy left when Walt died in 1966 of cancer. But not much could have left. He was the keeper of the flame and had to be the curator of the spirit that Walt Disney created.

He inherited the Disney entertainment empire. It was difficult for his neighbors in Windermere to grow accustomed to the fact that the little round, balding man with the twinkling eyes and inquisitive nature was the chairman of the board. But that's the way Roy Disney wanted it. That is the way he lived. He was a man of great personal warmth and charm, as personable as his late brother Walt.

Visiting the Magic Kingdom in 1971 was a unique experience for most of its guests who had never ventured to the West Coast to see Disneyland. Even the few guests who were familiar with Disneyland were taken aback by the massive scale of the Magic Kingdom and the blue skies that seemed to go on forever.

Over the decades, things were announced for WDW that never got built. Things that people assumed would last forever at WDW are no longer there. People who helped make Walt's final dream come true are sometimes forgotten. This section shares some of those stories as well as some additional hidden history of the Vacation Kingdom.

General Joe Potter

William E. "Joe" Potter was born in Oshkosh, Wisconsin, on July 17, 1905. He died of heart failure on December 5, 1988, in Orlando, Florida, at the age of 83.

As former president of Walt Disney Attractions Dick Nunis recalled in 1988 to the *Orlando Sentinel*:

> Joe was a man Walt Disney was very fond of. Without Joe Potter there would be no Walt Disney World today.

It was General Potter who got the land in central Florida prepared for building. (Admiral Joe Fowler then was in charge of construction on the property.) Potter oversaw the building of Walt Disney World entire infrastructure. He supervised the building and operation of the underground utilities and sewer, power, and water treatment plants that were considered revolutionary at the time.

He also developed drainage canals for the entire property, which were known affectionately as "Joe's ditches", and kept the water table constant. In an interview a year before his death, Potter joked:

> I went out and got three crackerjack college professors to show me how to do it. And then I got me another professor to help put the utilities underground.

During World War II, Potter directed logistical planning for the invasion of northern France, a transportation operation nicknamed "Red Ball Express". In 1956, President Dwight D. Eisenhower appointed Potter to serve as governor of the Panama Canal Zone.

At the end of his tenure as governor, and after 38 years with the army, Potter retired with the rank of major general in 1960. In his long career, he had been decorated with the Distinguished Service Medal, the Legion of Merit, the Bronze Star, and the Croix de Guerre.

Soon after his retirement from the army, he became executive vice president of the 1964–65 New York World's Fair, responsible for handling the construction of the federal and state attractions. These included 26 state pavilions and the $17 million United States pavilion.

At this time, he met Walt Disney (who had supplied attractions for four pavilions at the fair) who immediately realized that this was the man to be the vice president of his mysterious Florida Project and to prepare the land so it was suitable for construction.

"It didn't take you long to realize that Walt was a beginner of things, not a finisher," Potter said, meaning that Walt would spark the initial idea but depend on others to make it a reality.

Potter retired from Disney in 1974 as a senior vice president of Walt Disney World, as well as president of the board of supervisors of the Reedy Creek Improvement District. He later was president of Potter, Fowler and Associates Management Consultants and served on numerous civic and business boards, including the Greater Orlando Aviation Authority.

In 1976, he stated:

> I knew that we were going to have a project in Orlando many months before I joined Disney in September 1965. I had various functions. One was to establish the government, the Reedy Creek Improvement District. In that way, we were able to establish our own building department, develop our own building code, establish our own zoning, and do all of those things that are normally done by a county.
>
> You must realize that at the time Orange County did not have the facilities to examine plans for, let's say, a castle. No complicated buildings had been built in Orange County so the county, of course, was not staffed to examine plans and conduct the inspections requiring all buildings meet the safety and welfare specifications of those buildings.
>
> We spent an enormous amount of time planning things and dissecting them, "committeeing" them down darn near to death and then finally with approval, building them.

Richard F. Irvine

When Walt Disney World opened in 1971, the *Admiral Joe Fowler* riverboat plied the Rivers of America in Frontierland. It was joined in May 20, 1973, by the *Richard F. Irvine* riverboat.

The primary difference between the two ships was that the *Fowler* had two smokestacks, while the *Irvine* only had one. They both had three decks and a capacity of roughly 450 guests apiece. They were actual functioning steamboats, although on the Rivers of America they were guided by an I-beam underwater.

The original *Fowler* riverboat was damaged during a refurbishment at a backstage dry dock in 1980. It was broken up for scrap and in 1981 the *Irvine* in 1981 became the sole operating riverboat in the Magic Kingdom. In December 1982, the bell from the *Fowler* was installed on the *Roy O. Disney* steam train engine on the Walt Disney World railroad.

In 1996, the *Irvine* was completely refurbished and returned to service as the *Liberty Belle* riverboat. The name change was to theme it more closely to Liberty Square and make the name easier to remember.

Subsequently, in 1999, one of the ferries that transported guests across the Seven Seas Lagoon to the Magic Kingdom was re-christened *Richard F. Irvine* so as to continue to honor the late Imagineer's contributions while the other ferry was rechristened the *Admiral Joe Fowler*. (The third was a tribute to General Joe Potter.)

The *Irvine* had been named after Richard "Dick" Irvine who was born in Salt Lake City, Utah, on April 5, 1910. He moved with his family to southern California in 1922. Irvine was the son of a prominent Los Angeles ophthalmologist, Alexander Irvine, who was Walt Disney's personal eye doctor for years and was given a window on Disneyland's Main Street.

Irvine became an art director at 20th Century Fox and was hired by Walt in 1952 to act as liaison between Walt Disney Productions and an architectural firm that was being considered for designing Disneyland. He had previously worked at the Disney Studios as an art director on *Victory Through Airpower* (1943) and *The Three Caballeros* (1944), so he knew how Walt worked and the Disney culture.

Imagineer John Hench recalled:

> Because Dick had worked with movie set designs, creating structures and settings, he understood our needs more than standard architects.

Irvine headed design and planning for all Disneyland attractions, including significant contributions to the Haunted Mansion and Pirates of the Caribbean. At the 1964–65 New York World's Fair, he also guided the creation of such featured Disney attractions as "it's a small world".

He went on to help shape the master plan and attractions for Walt Disney World and, in 1967, was appointed executive vice president and chief operations officer of WED Enterprises (now Walt Disney Imagineering).

Concerning Walt Disney World, Irvine told author Bob Thomas:

> I often wonder how things would have been done differently if Walt had been alive. You know darn well it would have been entirely different from what we did do.

Before his death, Walt had put WED in charge of developing the theme park while he assembled a different group for the Epcot concept. Irvine was also involved in the creation and opening of California Institute of the Arts.

Irvine's heart condition and resulting illness prevented him from attending the opening of Walt Disney World. He retired in 1973 and passed away on March 30, 1976.

Irvine's daughter Maggie Irvine Elliot became the senior vice president of Creative Administration at WDI. His son married Kim Thomas (now Kim Irvine, currently an art director at WDI) who is also Imagineer Leota Toombs' daughter.

Thurl Ravenscroft

One of the most magical things that a Disney theme park accomplishes is to create an almost seamless experience for guests. The details are so correct and just right for the area that guests sometimes fail to notice them because those elements blend in so smoothly.

One of those details that is often ignored is the outstanding voice work provided in the attractions.

Thurl Ravenscroft, best known as the growling voice of Tony the Tiger for Kellogg's Frosted Flakes ("They're Grrrr—eat!") for over fifty years (beginning in 1952), had a rich and varied career as both an actor and a singer before his death at the age of 91 in May 2005.

Ravenscroft provided voice work for many Disney animated cartoons and Disney theme park attractions. As part of the musical group The Mellomen, he sang the theme songs for *Davy Crockett*, *Zorro*, and *Mickey Mouse Club* TV serials like *The Hardy Boys*.

Ravenscroft was the original on-board narrator on the Disneyland Railroad and Walt Disney Railroad, from their openings to around the year 2000 as the engines chugged around both magic kingdoms.

The Enchanted Tiki Room attraction has undergone changes at both parks over the decades. The voice of Fritz the German parrot was performed by Ravenscroft when the attraction first opened at both parks and is still heard there today after the latest rehabs. The Mellomen, including Ravenscroft, are part of the chorus on the song "The Tiki, Tiki, Tiki Room".

At Walt Disney World, when the Tropical Serenade was renamed The Enchanted Tiki Room, Under New Management, Ravenscroft (Fritz), Wally Boag (Jose), and Fulton Burley (Michael) all came back to the studio in 1997 to reprise their roles as the parrot hosts for the new show. Ernie Newton (Pierre) had passed away and was replaced by Jerry Orbach, whose French accent as Lumière in *Beauty and the Beast* (1991) had charmed audiences.

Shortly before his death, Ravenscroft said:

> They changed [the attraction] but they wanted to use the same cast. I was Fritz, the German parrot. And they called the four of us back but one of us had passed away. It was the French parrot. We got somebody else, but it was fun. Everybody in the studio came to see us perform. It was so wonderful.

Ravenscroft can be heard in many different locations in the Pirates of the Caribbean attraction. He is part of the group that sings "Yo Ho, Yo Ho, a Pirate's Life for Me". He is the voice of the drunken pirate leaning on a lamppost who is also singing along. In the trio of minstrels, Ravenscroft is the accordion player but, drawing on his experience from providing dog sounds for *Lady and the Tramp*, he is also the dog who is sitting nearby and howling along with the trio.

In the Haunted Mansion, Ravenscroft is singing the iconic "Grim Grinning Ghosts". He is one of the singing busts, the second from the left that has broken off its base (it's the one with the mustache most often mistaken for looking like Walt Disney). The others in the group are Chuck Schroeder, Bob Wright, Jay Myers, and Vern Rowe.

In Country Bear Jamboree (both the original Florida version and the later California version), Ravenscroft is the voice of Buff, the buffalo head on the wall.

Looking back on his nearly sixty-years of voice work for the Disney company, Ravenscroft said:

> Walt Disney was a wonderful man. I knew Walt personally through my work there, and it was a real treat. He knew exactly what he wanted, and he knew how it should be done. He was a charming, wonderful, warm man. I loved him.

Joe Rohde

Disney guests are fond of locating Hidden Mickeys, usually three circles that seem to resemble the face-front silhouette of Mickey Mouse. There are other, cleverer variations including Mickey's foot peeking out at the bottom of a poster in the Great Movie Ride.

Some Disney guests are so observant that they spot the names of people who worked on the parks that are hidden on props like crates, signs, and barrels. By the Jungle Cruise at the Magic Kingdom, for instance, you can find references to Bill Evans, Wathel Rogers, Winston Hibler, and Harper Goff, among others.

When Disney's Animal Kingdom opened, there were hidden references to various Imagineers throughout the park. The Shields hot air balloon trips refer to landscape planner John Shields. The architectural restoration company Mjafari is a shout-out to architect Ahmad Jafari.

However, as might be suspected, the most prominent name found throughout the park is that of Joe Rohde, the Imagineering executive designer and creative director for the project.

Rohde joined Imagineering in 1980 during the development of Epcot, contributing specifically to the Mexico Pavilion. He was later significantly involved in projects like the Adventurers Club on Pleasure Island, Disney Vacation Club Aulani Resort, and the Norway Pavilion.

During the tenth anniversary of Animal Kingdom, Rohde stated:

> My favorite memory of designing Disney's Animal Kingdom was walking and riding my bike in the African savanna in the days before we put the African animals in. The whole environment was completed and fully grown in. It went on forever and really looked, even smelled like Africa.
>
> There were thousands of frogs in the evening, and by day there were huge flocks of little grey doves that would burst out of the grass when

I walked by. Sometimes after work, I would just walk out and sit in the grass and it would be perfectly quiet.

My favorite parts of the park are the big savanna views of Kilimanjaro Safaris, the quieter parts of Maharajah Jungle Trek, and the Expedition Everest queue line.

My favorite memory of opening day was when Jane Goodall thanked all of us Imagineers for all of our dedication and hard work. The most unique contribution of DAK is the ongoing conservation program. This puts the idea of love of animals into real action in the real world.

Many advertisements in Harambe village are for Jorodi Masks & Beads. The name "Jorodi" is pronounced "Joe Rohde". Rohde supplied many exotic masks for the now defunct Adventurers Club.

Rohde would laugh that he traveled the world looking for artifacts for the club but couldn't find any that he felt would work, and so all the artifacts, even the African tribal masks, were obtained at swap meets in the Pasadena, California, area.

In the Adventurer's Club main show room, the crooked picture on the side of the stage included a caricature of Rohde as an adventurer in the right-hand side of the picture. It was just one of several Rohde references in the club.

The actual storefront for Jorodi Masks & Beads is hidden away on the second floor of the main room of Tusker House, over the hallway leading to the restaurant's restrooms. A sign there emphasizes the business specialized in earrings, a reference to the distinctively huge ones Rohde wears in his left ear that he gathered during his many travels.

The final sign in the queue for Expedition Everest states: "The Yeti Museum gratefully acknowledges the following individuals and organizations for their contributions of photographic material". Halfway down the second column on the left is the name Joe Rohde.

The signs for Cap'n Bob's Super Safaris in a hot-air balloon feature a caricature of Bob that looks very much like Rohde.

Rohde's presence is everywhere in the park he designed and maybe in some areas yet to be discovered by curious explorers.

Admiral Joe Fowler

In 1976, Admiral Joe Fowler recalled:

> They wanted to pave Main Street [at WDW] with old bricks. We were lucky enough to find a supply from brick streets being torn up in Winter Park. But the price they wanted was outrageous. We finally put the bricks on the side streets and paved Main Street with cement.

Fowler died at the age of 99 in his Bay Hill House in Florida on December 4, 1993.

Bob Mathieson, a former Walt Disney World executive vice president and friend of Fowler's, said:

> He had that great "can-do" spirit, and he lived it. He was truly, in every sense of the word, an officer and a gentleman.'

Fowler was a veteran of both world wars. He designed and built small gunboats during the 1920s and naval ships of all sizes during the 1930s and 40s, including the two biggest aircraft carriers of World War II, the *Lexington* and the *Saratoga*.

Fowler retired from the navy in 1948 with the rank of rear admiral. In 1952, he was brought back by President Harry Truman to direct the Federal Supply Management Agency, with orders to cut waste in the military.

Later, Walt Disney hired Fowler to consult on the building of the *Mark Twain* steamboat for Disneyland. Walt was so impressed that he put Fowler in charge on getting Disneyland constructed within a year. "Can do" was both Fowler's trademark attribute and his favorite expression.

Fowler recalled in a 1993 interview with the *Orlando Sentinel*:

> Walt said to me a couple of days after I was hired, "Now look, I will try to have the ideas, and you make the engineering realities of them."

Walt gave Fowler the task of planning and building the mysterious Florida Project which evolved into Walt Disney World. He was in charge of the construction and engineering, and was so instrumental in the park's construction he at one point held three positions: director of construction for Disney's Buena Vista Construction Company, senior vice president of engineering and construction for Walt Disney Productions, and chairman of the board of WED Enterprises, the former name of Walt Disney Imagineering.

Fowler recalled, in 1976:

> We built everything to withstand the force of a hurricane. That gave us a lot of problems with the design engineers. They were accustomed to designing for earthquakes at Disneyland. Now they had to design for hurricanes.
>
> Walt left a wonderful legacy with his trained art directors. [Imagineering President] Dick Irvine knew Walt would not permit anything to go ahead if he did not feel it was the ultimate, and the art directors held to this principle.
>
> We had to indoctrinate a lot of the contractors in the Disney tradition. We never had a real labor stoppage. There were some brief stoppages over who should do a particular job, but they were straightened out quickly.

Bob Matheison said in a 1993 interview with the *Orlando Sentinel*:

> Fowler was standing with Disney in the early days of Disneyland. They were looking at a performing stage that featured a waterfall, with a dressing room off to the side.
>
> 'Walt turned to Joe and said, "I'd like to part the water and let the entertainers come out, and then have the waterfall close behind them."
>
> Joe never batted an eye. 'He just said, "Can do, can do." I know he had no idea how he was going to part the water, but he said it without hesitation—"Can do." And, by golly, he went ahead and did it. He parted the water and closed it back up again.

Disney World International Airport

Walt Disney's original hand-drawn plans for the Florida property included many things that never were built, like a swamp ride. Those plans showed that Walt intended the property to have an operating international airport with at least three parallel runways on the land now roughly occupied by the city of Celebration. Walt referred to it as "the airport of tomorrow" in his famous short film explaining Epcot.

When Walt Disney World opened in 1971, there was no Orlando International Airport (not until 1976), just Orlando McCoy Jetport (which is why luggage tags for today's passengers still say "MCO" as the reference to that location) with its limited capacity.

With the expected influx of visitors, many of them from other countries, an "airport of tomorrow" had to be built today.

Roughly across the street from Walt's airport would be the primary entrance to the Epcot project or the main gate (which is why the non-descript building that houses Entertainment, Merchandising and Disney Design Group on Sherberth Road is known as "Main Gate", since that is where the planned entrance to the property was to be located).

Like Disneyland, Walt intended to control the crowds with just one entrance whether the guests arrived by car or by plane. A welcome center staffed by cast members who spoke different languages would be there at the entrance complex to assist foreign visitors.

By the completion of stage two of the Florida property by 1976, which would have included the addition of three new resorts near the Magic Kingdom and new attractions for the Magic Kingdom like Thunder Mesa with the Western River Expedition, it was expected that over four hundred people would be working at what was known as the Disney World airport.

By 1991, Disney projected that the airport would employ over two thousand full time workers and be surrounded by hundreds of motels accomodating the many travelers flying in and out during their visit to the Epcot area.

However, building such a facility would take several years, so a temporary area was built to handle guests who arrived at the existing Orlando airport and needed to get to the Magic Kingdom quickly. This short-take-off-and-landing runaway was built near the Magic Kingdom and was Florida's first STOLport facility able to handle up to four small propellor planes at a time.

There were never any plans for expansion of STOLport because, after all, this was meant as a temporary facility until the big international airport was built. But Disney could never get a major air carrier to partner with them in the costs for the larger airport, especially with the oil crisis in 1973. Delta Airlines came close at one point to signing on.

The continuing expansion of Orlando International Airport as well as drastic changes to the original plans for Epcot itself resulted in the large airport project quietly disappearing as an unneccessary expense.

Basically, when the Disney company abandoned the plans to build the Epcot city that Walt Disney envisioned, the airport was abandoned as well.

Former Imagineering executive Marty Sklar recalled:

> It made great sense to Walt, but he didn't live long enough to get into the nitty gritty details of getting an idea to work. There's a gigantic difference between the spark of a brilliant idea and the daily operation of an idea.

Roger Rabbit Toontown

As part of the plans for the infamous Disney Decade, one idea that had been discussed for Disneyland was to convert the area behind Main Street, USA into a Hollywood Land with a section devoted to Roger Rabbit that would feature some attractions.

In May 1991, Disney officially cancelled the project claiming in a statement to the *Los Angeles Times* that "proposed construction would come at the same time as development of the proposed Westcot theme park nearby" and the company wanted to focus on just one major project.

Wescot was later cancelled and evolved into Disney's California Adventure park.

These same Roger Rabbit elements that the Imagineers had developed were suggested for a planned expansion at the Disney-MGM Studios to be located in the approximate location of where Sunset Boulevard is today.

Known as Roger Rabbit's Hollywood (and sometimes as Maroon Studios, the fictitious animation studio where Roger works), it would have been an entire street that looked as if it belonged in Toontown with its wacky architecture.

Later versions of the concept had it reduced in size and located at the end of Sunset Boulevard near the current location of Rock 'n' Roller Coaster.

An often-quoted *New York Times* article described it as:

> This will be a kind of Toontown, where—as in the movie—only cartoon characters may live.

The street would be littered with all sorts of surprises like boxes of TNT, a grand piano dangling precariously over the street, and Roger-shaped holes in the walls. Red cars would take guests up and down the street, stopping at the Terminal Bar from the movie that would serve as the restaurant for the new area.

The Toontown Trolley attraction would have been a motion-control simulator like Star Tours with some differences including not only a screen in front but on each side of the cabin. There would be in-cabin effects like Roger-shaped dents when the character crashed into the roof during this madcap ride through Toontown.

Baby Herman's Runaway Baby Buggy would have been a traditional Fantasyland-like dark ride. Based on the incidents in the first Roger Rabbit theatrical short, *Tummy Trouble* (1989), where Roger and Baby Herman have a series of misadventures in a hospital, guests would board oversized baby buggy ride vehicles. They would careen down stairs, through hospital rooms, and around beds and patients.

When the attraction was described in the newspapers, some readers angrily complained that there was nothing funny about a hospital and that the Disney company was being insensitive to both patients (especially scared children) and doctors, especially since the short featured frightening sharp objects and scary mechanical devices.

Benny the Cab was an attraction planned for the area that did later get tweaked and built as Roger Rabbit's Car Toon Spin at Disneyland. Benny was transformed into his "twin cousin" Lenny. Imagineers tried to explain the missing Benny by saying that Roger was out driving him at the time so he was unavailable. In actuality, additional fees would have had to be paid to Amblin Entertainment for the use of the cab character.

Because of creative differences between Disney and Steven Spielberg and Amblin Entertainment, Roger Rabbit was removed from Disney theme parks by 1993. The Disney company philosophy became: why fight with Spielberg over the use of the character and share the revenues when there are dozens of new Disney animated characters, from a mermaid to a beast to an upcoming lion king, that guests love?

In 1994, Sunset Boulevard, an extension of the Hollywood of the 1940s, opened in the area instead, though some remnants of Roger's heyday as a character at the park can still be found.

Lake Buena Vista
New Orleans Square

Disney executive Dick Nunis, who oversaw the operation of both Disneyland and Walt Disney World, had a vision to expand the Disney Village Resort (now Disney Springs), which opened in May 1977 and featured the *Empress Lilly*, a re-creation of a 19th century paddle wheel steamboat.

Guests loved that the village was a quiet alternative to the Magic Kingdom and did not require an admission fee. It also became a popular spot for local residents.

Nunis told cast members in the May 1982 issue of *Eyes &Ears* cast newspaper:

> From the *Empress Lilly*, we're going into a New Orleans street, and you'll walk right into a beautiful New Orleans hotel.

The *Empress Lilly* restaurant would have been re-themed as not just a building that looked like a ship but a steamboat that had docked to unload its cargo and passengers at the riverfront town of New Orleans. Nearby there would be a new six-hundred room Disney hotel with the same French Quarter theme as New Orleans Square at Disneyland. A name for the hotel was never officially confirmed.

The guest rooms at the hotel would have been "hidden" in buildings resembling a cotton mill or a boatwright's shop. The rooms would be on the upper floors with the bottom floor reserved for shops and restaurants much like the design later used at the Boardwalk Resort.

An illustrated marketing packet was produced by the Disney company in September 1981 (later revised in April 1982) for what was called Lake Buena Vista New Orleans Square.

The lushly landscaped area, making use of already existing Florida flora, would have included approximately 120,000 square feet of restaurants, entertainment venues, and merchandise shops. The area would have been themed in an old New Orleans motif and would have rippled out from Royale Circle.

One of the restaurants was tentatively titled Garden Restaurant with one façade facing the *Empress Lilly*, looking like a Southern mansion, and a different façade facing the lagoon. As at Disneyland, there would also have been a Café Orleans with Cajun- and Creole-inspired cuisine in a casual setting.

The entertainment venues would have included a Preservation Hall Jazz Lounge. Jazz artists had already been performing periodically at the Village Restaurant to such popularity that a cover charge had to be instituted. A more raucous time was had at the full bar in the Baton Rouge Lounge of the *Empress Lilly* that featured Dixieland Jazz.

An intriguing mystery was that one of the exterior designs for a building in the brochure was reminiscent of the exterior of the Pirates of the Caribbean attraction at Disneyland even though that ride was already in existence at the Magic Kingdom.

A New Orleans-themed resort, named Port Orleans, did open on Walt Disney World property on May 17, 1991, thanks to Fugleberg Koch Architects of Winter Park, Florida, in collaboration with the Disney Development Company.

Themed to the French Quarter of New Orleans around the mid-1800s, it was situated by the Sassagoula River, a man-made Disney waterway named after the Native American word for the Mississippi River. The resort was characteristic of the New Orleans French Quarter with balconies, wrought iron railings, cobblestone streets, and courtyards, but with Disney touches like jazz-playing alligators leading guests to the pool area.

On March 1, 2001, the resort officially merged with Dixie Landings and became Port Orleans: French Quarter (with Dixie Landings becoming Port Orleans: Riverside).

Yesterday Hotel

In 1967, the Imagineers created a full-color map to indicate the various resort hotels that would surround the Magic Kingdom theme park. The hotels were to be self-contained themed experiences with every element reinforcing the main theme. Placeholder names were given to these possible hotels.

The map showed Cape Cod Village, Yesterday Hotel (to be the first Disney resort hotel located inside a park), Frontier Village, Spanish Colonial Hotel, Oriental Motel, Dutch Hotel, and African Hotel (to theme in with Adventureland).

In place of Disneyland's famed Opera House, the Magic Kingdom had what is now called the Town Square Theater. When the Magic Kingdom opened in 1971, that beautiful building was officially the elegant Main Street Hotel that housed the Gulf Hospitality Center. Dorothea Redmond had created concept art for the possibility of building an actual upscale Victorian hotel on Main Street.

The hotel would not only have encompassed the actual building as it is today but expanded into the backstage area that became a cast member parking lot.

Some of those design elements for an actual hotel still remain, including the individual balconies on the upper-floor windows and the broad front porch with rocking chairs.

Since the Disney company had never operated a hotel and the development of plans for an elaborate series of nearby themed hotels beginning with the Contemporary and the Polynesian had become overwhelming, the idea of an in-park hotel was put on hold.

According to the original storyline, the hotel was located next to the train station so that people would have a place to stay while they waited for their train connection or while visiting the city.

When the Magic Kingdom opened in 1971, this beautiful building became the Hospitality Center, the unofficial central location for all of Walt Disney property, where guests could make reservations for resort rooms, dinner shows, golfing, and other recreational activities.

The large, polished wooden counter was primarily staffed by friendly and attractive young women who extolled the virtues of Gulf Oil, the sponsor, and handed out maps and brochures that assisted guests with driving routes, suggesting places to visit in central Florida, and selecting hotels or motels at which to stay on their trip.

In addition to the service stations located on the property for both guests and employees, Gulf Oil had exclusive rights for oil products used on the property as it did at Disneyland.

"Etched glass doors, potted palms, comfortable velvet settees and antique chairs set the mood for relaxation and comfort," claimed the 1972 "Gulf Personal Tourguide (sic) to Walt Disney World", describing the Hospitality Center. Fixtures like the interior counter suggested a turn-of-the-century hotel lobby.

The hotel was to be a full-sized building rather than one using forced perspective because it was necessary to block the guests' view of the Contemporary Resort, which would have conflicted with the theme of Main Street. The Contemporary was still clearly visible in Tomorrowland because it had a vaguely futuristic look that didn't detract from the "world of the immediate future" theme.

The Hospitality Center officially closed March 1990 and became Disneyana Collectibles. It became the Town Square Exposition Hall in 1998 and closed in 2011. It was then re-themed as the Town Square Theater.

Muppet Studios

Muppet Studios (also known as Muppet Movieland) was intended to be a separate land at the back of Disney-MGM Studios. Phase One was to include Jim Henson's Muppet*Vision 3D, a parade down Hollywood Boulevard, live stage shows called Meet the Muppets and Muppets on Location: Days of Swine and Roses, and a merchandise shop themed to the stage set of the Happiness Hotel from the movie *The Great Muppet Caper* (1981).

Imagineer Mark Eades told me:

> Jim Henson was very involved with the project. He was genuinely interested in doing theme park attractions. I think Jim liked that it would be something people could see for a long time in an environment like a Disney theme park. I think he also liked doing something new, unique and groundbreaking.

Henson's unexpected death in 1990 and his failure to sign a contract with Disney turning over control of The Muppets led to a dispute with the Henson family and the Muppet Studios expansion was cancelled.

Mama Melrose's restaurant was originally intended to be an eatery called The Great Gonzo's Pizza Pandemonium Parlor, operated by Gonzo and Rizzo the Rat. Things would constantly be going horribly (and amusingly) wrong, both offstage and in the dining area itself.

Gonzo and Rizzo would have hired the Swedish Chef to run the kitchen. Overhead television monitors would have shown the antics in the kitchen as food fought back against being prepared.

The inside walls would have been decorated with Muppet memorabilia (both real and created), just like the famous Planet Hollywood restaurant. The place would also be interactive—at any moment the kitchen doors might explode open in a cloud of chicken feathers and rants from the chef. Rizzo and his friends (with the help of the serving staff) would deliver meals to the tables on a small model railroad train with flat cars that ran throughout the restaurant.

The Backlot Theater was originally intended as the location for the major attraction at the Muppet Studios, the Great Muppet Movie Ride, a parody of the park's premiere attraction announced spring 1993.

Jim Henson explained it as "a backstage ride explaining how movies were shot ... and all the information is wrong". Audio-animatronics Muppets would find themselves in classic film scenes including the 1931 *Frankenstein* where Miss Piggy and Kermit have stumbled into the lab of Dr. Bunsen Honeydew trying to bring life to a ten-foot tall Beaker with bolts sticking out of his neck.

Pigs in Space would have had Link Hogthrob, Dr. Julius Strangepork, and Miss Piggy in the middle of a battle with space "pie-rats" (pirates who are Rizzo the rat and his relatives). Both groups are wildly blasting lasers as the rodents try to swing across on ropes to board the spaceship.

Peter Pan would have been parodied with Kermit (as Peter). Rat technicians clearly operate the awkward and obvious pulley rigs and ropes to help these performers fly. However, the robust Miss Piggy dressed as Tinker Bell is difficult to control so there are huge holes in the scenery.

The area outside the attraction, especially the stores, would have had Muppet themes. Philo's Fish Co. was originally intended to be Lew Zealand's Boomerang Fish Market. Guests walking along the street would have heard the performer practicing. In the windows would have been fish packed in ice that would spin around or offer awful puns like being "hard of herring".

One of the few remnants of the Muppet Studios is in the pre-show area of Muppet*Vision 3D, where crates are clearly addressed to be delivered to the same destination: Muppet Studios, not Muppet Labs. In early 2004, the Disney company finally purchased the complete rights to the Muppets.

Germany Rhine River Cruise

The United Kingdom, Italy, Japan, and Germany pavilions in World Showcase at Epcot all had planned attractions that were eliminated by opening day, primarily for budgetary reasons as well as rapidly approaching deadlines preventing them from being finished on time.

The 1982 book *Walt Disney's EPCOT* by Richard Beard provides this brief description of the proposed Rhine River Cruise attraction that was supposed to be inside the Germany Pavilion:

> The future River Ride promises to be as enjoyable as it is informative. An early concept has visitors boarding a "cruise boat" for a simulated ride down the Rhine and other rivers, the trip affording a visual impression in miniature of the cultural heritage of Germany's past and the highlights of its present. Among the detailed (miniature) models envisioned are scenes in the Black Forest, the Oktoberfest, Heidelberg, the industrial Ruhr Valley ... the possibilities are limited only by the planners' imaginations.

The description in the Walt Disney Productions 1976 annual report stated the attraction would be:

> ...a cruise down Germany's most famous rivers—the Rhine, the Tauber, the Ruhr and the Isar. Detailed miniatures of famous landmarks will also be seen including one of the Cologne Cathedral.

Busch Gardens of Williamsburg, Virginia, had a Rhine River Cruise from its opening in 1975, but it was primarily a slow ride for guests to enjoy the park's beautiful landscaping.

Another concept was proposed by the Imagineers to make the ride less like a German version of Disneyland's leisurely Storybook Land attraction and more exciting, with characters and scenes based on German composer Richard Wagner's epic opera *Der Ring des Nibelungen*.

Siegfried would have received the magical ring made from Rhine gold for his killing of Fafner the dragon. Valkyries led by Brunnhilde would have appeared. The conclusion of the attraction would have been a water plunge through the fabled caves of gold.

The entrance to the original proposed attraction would have been through huge archways at the back of the pavilion where guests would have encountered large wooden doors. That area contains a large mural of Sommerfest today. Entering through the doorway, guests would have gone through a queue to a loading area for the boats.

Guests in the boats would all have been seated facing toward the right side with the show scenery directly in front of them. Behind them would have been dark walls. This decision helped keep costs down as well as directing the guests' attention to exactly where Imagineers wanted them to look.

The unload area would have given guests a glimpse of the restaurant and the live entertainment on the Biergarten stage to tempt them to go inside.

Part of the show building was built, including flumes cut into concrete where the boats would have traveled. When that building was eventually completed later, it was used as rehearsal rooms and storage.

The Japan show building meant to house the Meet the World attraction that moved to Tokyo Disneyland instead was completely built and that empty area has been used for a variety of purposes.

Meet the World was a four-act show similar to Carousel of Progress except that the audience would be seated on a rotating turntable facing outward rather than inward, allowing the stages to be larger. In each scene there was a movie screen on the back wall so both movies and audio-animatronics were integrated, as in The American Adventure.

The show, which ran from April 15, 1983, to June 20, 2002, at Tokyo Disneyland had a magical talking crane taking two children from Yokohama on a trip through time to see Japan's colorful history, from its volcanic beginning to early trading with other nations, isolationism, and finally the reopening of the country. The song between each scene was written by the Sherman Brothers.

First Families of Walt Disney World

A tradition started at Disneyland on July 18, 1955, was to pick a "first family" to be honored as the first official guests to enter a Disney theme park and to reward them with lifetime passes. That same tradition continued at Walt Disney World when the Magic Kingdom opened on October 1, 1971.

The lucky sandy-haired father was William "Bill" Windsor Jr. from nearby Lakeland, Florida, who was accompanied by his pretty blue-eyed wife, Marty, and their sons Jay, who was 3 years old, and Lee, who was nearly 19 months old. It turned out they had arrived so early that the entire family had slept in their car overnight at the nearest roadside rest area in order to be among the first into the parking lot.

For the opening of Epcot on October 1, 1982, Richard and Paula Cason and their four children (Jennifer, 16; Chris, 15; Ricky, 14; and Jody, 13) were the first family. They were from Winter Park and got up at 4:30am to arrive at the park at 6:00am only to find the gates wouldn't open to the parking lot until 7:00am.

Cason said he "drove around the loop" before finally making it into the parking lot. "I just told the kids to get out and run for the gate," he told reporters at the opening ceremonies. They received a silver pass from Card Walker, the chairman and CEO of Walt Disney Productions.

Due to limited space, only the first family, Walker, the press, and a handful of invited guests were allowed inside the gates to witness the opening ceremony. All the other guests that morning were kept outside and only saw the festivities on that evening's newscasts.

For the opening of Disney-MGM Studios on May 1, 1989, the official first family was Allan and Mary Guiterrz (both 37) and their teen daughters Gina (16) and Dawn (14), along with Mary's father Marshall Busser (61) from York, Pennsylvania. They waited six hours.

Allan was a carpenter and Mary a postal worker and part-time belly dancer. They were greeted by Michael Eisner and Bob Hope who escorted them down Hollywood Boulevard. They commented that they were spending so much time with interviews that they worried they might not have time to see the park before they had to leave.

For the opening of Disney's Animal Kingdom on April 22, 1998, 350 cars were waiting in the parking plaza by 5:00am. The park was scheduled to open at 7:00am, but there was such a crush of guests that Disney opened an hour earlier after a short ceremony that featured the song "Circle of Life" from the movie *The Lion King* (1994) and then had to close the park again 75 minutes later.

The first guests through the gate were Brenda Herr of St. Petersburg, Florida, her husband, Damon Chepren, and their twenty-two month old son, Devon, who had all slept for only two hours the night before cramped in a Mazda 626 to ensure a spot at the front of the line. Chepren said:

> She [Brenda] was determined, and she let me know darn well we were going to make it happen. When we were waiting in the car, she looked me in the eyes and said, "You *will* run".

DAK also paid tribute to the first "honorary first family", Michael Werikhe and his daughters, Acacia, 9, and Kora, 7, in a ceremony at the park's Conservation Station. Werikhe was known throughout the world as Rhino Man, for his one-man crusade to boost public awareness of the plight of the black rhinoceros. Roy E. Disney presented Werikhe with a giant key of life, in the shape of the Tree of Life, the park's massive icon. In addition, Walt Disney World made a contribution in support of Werikhe's conservation work.

WDW's First Disneyana Convention

Two West Coast Disney fan organizations, the Mouse Club and the National Fantasy Fan Club (now called the Disneyana Fan Club), held three-day weekend Disney conventions in Anaheim, California, for many years beginning in 1982. Several hundred fans from around the country attended.

The popularity (and the financial rewards) of those conventions did not go unnoticed by the Disney company. During September 24–27, 1992, Disney held its first Disneyana convention at Walt Disney World's Contemporary Resort in Orlando.

In his welcoming speech, the chairman of Disney Attractions, Dick Nunis, said:

> Welcome to our first "official" Disneyana convention. Now, we know this is not the "first" Disneyana convention, but as Walt Disney once said, "There is no new idea in the world we live in…. What you do is take a good one and improve on it." So, we try to do that.

Later, in a special presentation, he reminisced about his career using audio and video clips of Walt Disney as well as talking about the building of Walt Disney World.

The Disneyana convention was a major production with over 800 people and an elaborate attendee package (including a watch and a special pewter medallion sculpted by Marc Delle of the Disneyana convention logo) as well as limited-edition merchandise that quickly sold out.

On Thursday evening, at an ice cream social at the Contemporary, original Mouseketeers Bobby Burgess, Sharon Baird, and Sherri Alberoni autographed photographs at a façade of the Mouseketeer clubhouse.

On Friday, Dick Nunis drove up with Mickey Mouse in the LiMOUSEine. Guests attended the official opening ceremony in the Fantasia Ballroom. Jack Wagner, the voice of Disney, was the emcee, reminding guests there was no photography or videotaping because "this special performance is for your eyes only".

The speakers included landscaper Bill Evans, Max Howard (director of Disney Feature Animation Florida), Bo Boyd (president of Disney Consumer Products) and Ester Ewert of Disney Art Editions.

The afternoon had a limited edition sale and artist signing, a Disneyana fair selling signs and props, a Disney Business Group presentation (with displays by everyone from the Disney Channel to the Disney Vacation Club to the Disney Classics Collection), and a Disneyana trade show with independent dealers. The day finished with a Disneyana auction where an original individual Dumbo ride vehicle from Disneyland sold for $16,000.

On Saturday, Dave Smith and Robert Tieman were delivered to the convention in an armored truck for their presentation of thirty treasures from the Walt Disney Archives.

Imagineer Tony Baxter talked about Euro Disneyland and Admiral Joe Fowler enthralled the crowd even though he was in his 90s. That afternoon, the general public was allowed to join the conventioneers at various fairs and trade shows to spend their money. However, only the conventioneers got to attend that night's banquet that finished with the Kids of the Kingdom performing "The Best of Disney".

The 1993 convention was held in Anaheim, California. The Disneyana conventions hosted by Disney ended in 2003 and there is still speculation about the reasons for its demise. One Disney leader pointed out that while the convention made a healthy profit, it did not make an "obscene profit", meaning that the time, labor, and resources could be re-allocated to something like pins and generate more income with less effort for the Disney company.

The D23 Expo event, begun in September 2009, has taken the place of the Disneyana conventions.

Pardoned Turkeys

Both the Disneyland and Walt Disney World petting zoos have been homes for presidential pardoned Thanksgiving turkeys.

The first officially pardoned Thanksgiving turkey was in 1989 during President George H.W. Bush's first Thanksgiving in office, although informally some other Thanksgiving and Christmas turkeys had been given stays of execution by previous chief executives. For instance, President John F. Kennedy casually spared a turkey on November 19, 1963, just days before his assassination, and sent it back so it could continue to grow. However, it was not an official pardon.

Most people have assumed President Truman began the practice of pardoning the turkey, thanks to a photo of the president with a turkey. The Harry S. Truman Presidential Library and Museum in Independence, Missouri, has pointed out that "[t]he poultry board gave [Truman] turkeys every year and we think they probably ended up on the dinner table". There is no documentation that Truman ever pardoned any of the birds, but that is the popular myth.

At some point, the birds who escaped a White House dinner were sent off to petting zoos and, beginning in 2005, they were sent to the Big Thunder Ranch at Disneyland. The first pardoned turkey to be sent to Walt Disney World was in 2007.

On November 20, 2007, in a ceremony at the White House Rose Garden, President George W. Bush pardoned two turkeys, one named May and the other Flower (together, Mayflower) and said they would be "flown to Disney World, where they will serve as honorary grand marshals for the Thanksgiving Day Parade. May they live the rest of their lives in blissful gobbling."

Both birds got a first-class flight to Orlando on a United Airlines jet and a red-carpet entry to the theme park. WDW spokesperson Duncan Wardle said that this tied in with Disney's "What's next?" advertising campaign featuring a star football player after each Super Bowl:

I think, if the turkey could speak, he'd say he's "going to Disney World".

Each year, the National Turkey Federation works with different farmers to send two birds to the White House. One will be pardoned, and the other is a backup. Neither is ever really at risk of winding up on the First Family's dinner table.

Keith Williams, spokeman for the National Turkey Federation, explained:

> Everyone calls it "the pardon", but it's the presentation of the national Thanksgiving turkey. I believe it was George H. W. Bush who made an offhand comment that he was going to pardon the turkey, and that's where it became a custom.

After a while, Disney no longer wanted the turkeys nor the responsibility associated with them.

Dean Norton, the director at Mount Vernon in charge of livestock, said:

> The birds are fed in such a way to increase their weight. [Americans] want a nice big breasted turkey and so they are fed high protein diets and they get quite large. The organs, though, that are in this bird are meant for a smaller bird. They just can't handle the extra weight, so they end up living not as long [as wild turkeys]. Often they are dead within a year of being pardoned.

Beginning in 2010, the pardoned turkeys were sent to George Washington's Mount Vernon estate and starting in 2013 they have been sent to Turkey Hill Farm in Morven Park in Virginia.

Walt Disney World Christmas Parade

The Walt Disney World Very Merry Christmas Parade was broadcast live from Walt Disney World for the first time in December 1983 with television personalities Joan Lunden and Mike Douglas serving as hosts. The early broadcasts were ninety minutes long, becoming two hours long in 1988, the first year there was a simulcast from Disneyland. In recent years, the show has been trimmed to an hour.

Lunden, well known for her role as co-host of ABC's *Good Morning America*, show continued to be the primary host for the parade on television for over a decade. In 1986, she told *Orlando Sentinel* reporter Jay Bobbin:

> I *love* doing it. I'm looking forward to having my family with me so I can become a Disney World tour guide, which is a job I'd be very adept at.

In 1984, Bruce Jenner was Lunden's co-host and Regis Philbin popped up for the first time in a few segments as a roving commentator on the street, a role he continued until 1991. He would do special segments as well, including a "hard hat" tour of the Grand Floridian Resort and Disney-MGM Studios in the 1987 show.

In 1985 and 1986, Lunden hosted with dancer Ben Vereen. Then, from 1987-1990, it was Lunden with co-host Alan Thicke. In 1991, Regis finally came in off the street and joined Lunden at her side as the co-host and continued to do so up through the 1995 parade.

In 1996, Suzanne Somers and Jerry Van Dyke did the emcee duties, followed in 1997 by Melissa Joan Hart and Ben Savage, and in 1998 by Caroline Rhea and Richard Kind.

It wasn't until 2001 that Regis Philbin and Kelly Ripa hosted from the center of Town Square on Main Street, USA and continued to do so until 2009. The 2005 edition of the parade, hosted by that duo, won Harborlight Entertainment and ABC the daytime Emmy award for Outstanding Special Class Special.

In December 2009, Regis, recovering from hip surgery, was absent from the festivities. Ryan Seacrest, reporting from California, joined Kelly Ripa and Nick Cannon, who were in Florida. This was also the year that the show's name was changed to its new title, Disney Parks Christmas Day Parade. By 2010, Seacreast and Nick Cannon had become the hosts.

Mario Lopez, Maria Menounos (who had also appeared the previous year), and Nick Cannon hosted in 2011 and 2012, with Neil Patrick Harris joining Cannon in 2013. Rob Mariano and Robin Roberts (with Sarah Hyland at Aulani) hosted the 2014 festivities.

In 2000, a parade special was not aired on Christmas Day. Instead a "Tracking Santa" Christmas Eve show was produced. For 2014, the show was renamed the Disney Parks Frozen Christmas Celebration, and then renamed again for 2015 as the Disney Parks Unforgettable Christmas Celebration, hosted by Robin Roberts and Jesse Palmer.

The parade was last broadcast live in 1996. It had always been broadcast live on Christmas Day, usually on CBS, with whom Disney had partnered for Thanksgiving and New Year celebrations as well, until Disney bought out ABC in 1996. However, it was determined that there were too many negative variables, from inclement weather to performers not being able to appear on that particular day, so that it was more reasonable to pre-tape the event to guarantee a good show. The taping usually takes place over two days sometime during November or even as late as early December.

During the taping, floats are frequently stopped and restarted and performers repeat their routines several times. Guests on Main Street and in front of the castle are encouraged to cheer and applaud loudly, sometimes at nothing, just to get a reaction shot for the cameras.

For many family households, watching the Disney Parks Christmas Celebration became a tradition over the thirty-plus years it has aired on television.

Why Walt Disney World Is Not In St. Louis

From 1963 into 1964, Walt Disney was in discussions with the city of St. Louis to build a five story building covering over two city blocks that would house an indoor entertainment complex called Riverfront Square.

The complex would include a pirate's lair and blue bayou boat ride (later combined at Disneyland into Pirates of the Caribbean), a haunted house, a Circarama 360 theater, a Mike Fink ride, a Lewis and Clark Adventure ride, and even a Mississippi steamboat attraction.

Since it would be an enclosed area devoted to telling the story of the state of Missouri, the Mississippi River, and Mark Twain, Walt had plans to create his own "sky" on the ceiling that would simulate weather and time of day so that the venue could operate year round in a climate-controlled environment.

Walt insisted that no alcohol be served in the indoor venue because he wanted it to be family friendly and without alcohol it would keep out what Walt referred to as "rowdies" who would disrupt the experience. It was the same philosophy he had at Disneyland.

Admiral Joe Fowler who was in charge of construction for both Disneyland and Walt Disney World was 82 years old in 1988 and living in Florida at his Bay Hill home when he shared this story with me:

> Well, it seems almost from the day Disneyland was opened people were after Walt to open another. If not exactly like the one in California, then something else, but hurry up and build *something*. Walt resisted this at first, but then, after our New York World's Fair exhibits were in place and proving a spectacular success, he began to look around the country.
>
> I think it was in early 1964 that after several visits, Walt gave the green light for some preliminary theme park work to start in St. Louis.

We were invited to this fancy civic banquet, where there were lots of enthusiastic bankers, chamber of commerce types, the mayor and his people, that kind of thing.

At some point well into the dinner, August Busch (owner of Anheuser-Busch brewery and a powerful man in St. Louis) stood up when he should have sat down and said something to the effect of "Any man who would build something like this, and then not serve beer and liquor inside ought to have his head examined."

Now Walt, when in public, didn't show much emotion if he got angry. He would just remain quiet where usually he was quite talkative. But when you saw his left eyebrow shoot up, you knew there was a serious state of affairs. Well, when Walt heard that Busch considered him crazy for not selling alcohol in the thing, his eyebrow arched straight up.

Once we were all on the company plane and headed back to California, Walt gathered us for a meeting and said, "All right, forget about St. Louis." Nobody had to ask why. The bankers called, all upset that we had pulled out. Some even visited us later, but it was to no avail. After that Walt said maybe we should concentrate more on Florida.

When we picked up the bulk of 27,000 acres in Florida, Walt was delighted but not overwhelmed or over the moon. If he had had his way, we would have bought 50,000 acres!

Interestingly, documentation has been uncovered in recent years that Walt did not consider the St. Louis project as an alternative to his interest in building something in Florida. He intended to do both things simultaneously.

The biggest issue was not the selling of alcohol but that St. Louis felt that Disney was going to pay for the entire thing itself whereas Walt felt that St. Louis was going to finance it and then later be reimbursed from the net profits of the operation but that the property would be owned solely by Disney.

In any case, on July 13, 1965, St. Louis officials and Disney executives jointly announced that the project would not be built. Four months later in, November 1965, Disney made a public announcement of the plans to build in Florida.

Disney Dollars

The Disney company retired without warning its Disney Dollars program on Saturday May 14, 2016. Existing Disney Dollars will continue to be accepted for purchases since they never expire. Disney Dollars are real legal tender and can be exchanged for their U.S. equivalent at Disneyland and Walt Disney World with certain restrictions.

Disney marketing executive Jack Lindquist decided that Disney theme parks provided services to more people over the years than a small country and so should have their own currency. In his autobiography, *In Service to the Mouse,* he wrote:

> Part of my thinking when I started this process was that the public would have more fun using Disney money in Disneyland and they could turn the money in when they left the park, or they could keep it to use anytime they came back (just like the previous attraction ticket coupons).

Disney Dollars were first available in a one-dollar denomination with a waving Mickey Mouse on the front and the Fantasyland castle on the back and in a five-dollar denomination with a dignified Goofy posing on the front and a steamboat on the back. They were illustrated by Matt Mew of Disney's Creative Services and were redeemable for goods or services at Disneyland.

The currency was first released at Disneyland on May 5, 1987 (and could only be used at Disneyland; beginning September 9, the Disneyland bills could be used at Walt Disney World as well) and at Walt Disney World beginning October 2, 1987.

For the first year, state-of-the-art four-color printing was provided by Embossing Printers Inc. of Battle Creek, Michigan.

The bills went through a complex intaglio engraving process that gave them a raised texture and fine detail. U.S. Banknote Corporation of Chicago, noted for designing stock certificates, bank notes, bonds, and other security documents, handled this part of the process.

Disney Dollars were produced with the same level of "care and concern as any other currency," Lindquist said.

Since September 1987, bills for Disneyland are classified as the "A" series and the ones for Walt Disney World are labeled "D". That first year, the images were identical. For the inaugural run, over two million dollars worth of Disney Dollars was put into circulation, or approximately 870,000 individual bills.

In November 1989, a ten dollar bill was added for both series featuring Minnie Mouse, making her the first female to appear on paper currency issued in the United States.

In 1992, the Disney Stores started accepting the bills, as did the Disney Cruise Line when it started in 1998.

Occasionally, special Disney Dollar were issued such as a one-dollar bill in 1993 to celebrate Mickey Mouse's 65th birthday.

The intent was that most people who bought the bills would never redeem them for their face value but rather save them as an inexpensive souvenir or collect the different variations that came out each year.

New Disney dollars have been produced every year since 1987 except in 1992, 2004, 2010, 2011, and 2012. Every Disney Dollar issued in nearly three decades included Scrooge McDuck's signature as treasurer and an image of Tinker Bell on the front side.

In addition, Disney Dollars were meant to discourage guests from using actual money (just like the original A–E tickets) so they would not consciously be aware of how much things were costing. Disney Dollars were actually considered more like gift certificates than currency.

Like vintage attraction tickets, the souvenir value of Disney Dollars now that they are no longer being produced exceeds the face monetary value of the actual bill and eBay listings have these collectibles at several times their original cost.

Disney gift cards are cheaper and easier to produce and, at least for now, will still remain in existence.

The Mickey Mouse Tax

One of the surprises that did not happen for Walt Disney World's 20th anniversary in 1991 was the Mickey Mouse tax. I suspect most Walt Disney World fans have no clue whatsoever about this blip in Disney history.

The Florida State Senate proposed a Mickey Mouse state license plate celebrating Walt Disney World's 20th anniversary because there was the potential to make millions of dollars for the state.

On the left hand side of the plate would be Mickey Mouse in his tuxedo leaping out with hands outstretched from the zero in the number twenty. On his head would be a coned-shaped striped birthday hat. In the background would be the silhouette of Cinderella Caste and colorful confetti streamers would be all over the plate. At the top would be the word "Florida" and at the bottom the words "Years of Magic".

This special plate reading "20 Years of Magic" would cost people seventeen dollars more than regular license plates, and in return for giving up the profits on the plate, Disney would gain goodwill and free publicity. Another deciding factor for Disney was that the estimated seven million dollars in profits would help pay for one of then Florida Governor Lawton Chiles' pet projects: health care for poor pregnant women and their children.

In fact, it was Disney itself that first presented the idea to the Florida Senate, but many representatives took up the cause enthusiastically.

Oddly, it was the governor himself who was not in love with the idea. "We don't like the Mickey Mouse tax," stated Mary Jane Gallagher, the communications director for Chiles.

Appropriations Chairman Ron Saunders (a Democrat from Key West) concurred:

> The House doesn't like it either. I don't think we're really taking it too seriously.

Representative Vernon Peeples, a Democrat from Punta Gorda who fought hard against the bill for the license tag, saying that it was just free advertising for the Disney company, added:

> If the House approves the bill, we will all look goofy.

Senate Appropriations Chairman Winston "Bud" Gardner (whose son was a Disney artist) countered that in a year where legislators were scrambling to find money to pay for schools and health care, Disney's offer was more than generous and welcome.

Initially, Michael Eisner didn't care for the idea either when it was first proposed at the beginning of 1991. Gardner explained:

> [Eisner] has a very strong protectiveness of the Disney characters. It was only when people came to talk about children's programs that he got interested. He said all the proceeds have to be used for children.

Orange Country Commissioner Bill Donegan (who had previously been critical of Walt Disney World and its relationship with Florida) said he liked the idea of the license plates:

> I think Disney looks at this as goodwill. Those license plates crank out a heck of a lot of money and it will go to a worthy cause. Nothing Disney does, does not have an ulterior motive. It'll be good for Disney. It'll be good for Florida. They just need to keep an eye on where the money is going.

The House refused to consider the proposal. In a rare move that threatened to hold up the legislature's adjournment, House representatives voted 65-52 against a bill needed to implement the $29.3 billion budget because they opposed the section about the Disney license plate.

So the project died.

However, Disney quietly arranged that during the 20th celebration, for every souvenir license plate that was sold in the Disney theme parks for five dollars, two of those dollars would go to Healthy Start, the state program for poor pregnant women and children.

Florida Neverlands, Part One

The huge success of Walt Disney World inspired the announcement and the building of many other entertainment venues in the central Florida area that quickly disappeared. Among them:

Circus World was a theme park built near Haines City, Florida, near the intersection of US 27 and Interstate 4. Owned and operated by Ringling Brothers and Barnum & Bailey Circus, it was also intended to become winter headquarters for the circus. The park opened in 1974 and, during its first two years, added several attractions, including a carousel, a wooden roller coaster, and a Ferris wheel, in addition to live shows. It closed in 1986.

Boardwalk and Baseball was at the same location as the previously defunct Circus World. Owned and operated by Harcourt Brace Jovanovich, it opened on February 14, 1987, and closed January 17, 1990. While the area was themed to baseball, the park recycled some of the existing rides from Circus World.

Splendid China was a theme park near Orlando that opened in 1993 and closed on December 31, 2003. The park was 75 acres with more than 60 replicas at one-tenth scale. Each piece was handcrafted to maintain authenticity, and included landmarks like the Great Wall, the Temple of Heaven, the Temple of Confucius, the Summer Palace, and Three Ancient Pagodas in Dali, as well as more than 50 other buildings. The attraction was surrounded by controversy because of the direct involvement of the Chinese government in its operation. Once the park closed, it was victimized by vandals stealing the miniatures or parts of them. The park was officially demolished in 2013.

A few other projects heralded with great fanfare but never built were:

DestiNations Theme Park and Resort was announced on May 16, 2005 by Paidia Parks. According to the official press release:

Paidia's DestiNations Theme Park and Resort will be a celebration of the beauty of our world. We seek to bring the world's most exotic and exciting places together and put them within reach, and at the very heart and essence of our mission is the quest for peace and hope through the understanding and appreciation of the many diverse cultures on Earth.

The park would focus on the cultural and natural wonders of the most exotic and diverse reaches of the world: Egypt, Thailand, Peru, Russia, and New Zealand. It would be educational and family friendly and supposedly have plenty of thrilling rides, shows, and attractions.

For the first time at a theme park, DestiNations would offer a "mild or wild" pass so that guests with limitations of age, height, physical restrictions, or other issues would be able to "share the same experience without the bumps and jostles that may cause discomfort."

DestiNations was planned for a 430-acre parcel west of Kissimmee, once earmarked for Doug Henning's never built Vedaland theme park. In addition to the 140-acre theme park, the land would be used for a 1,000-unit condominium and fractional resort with nearly 200,000 square feet of retail space. The group also looked at the old Splendid China location.

When initial funding in excess of $300 million could not be raised, the project was abandoned.

Hurricane World was supposed to be both a serious hurricane research center and a tourist attraction featuring giant simulated storms.

Roy Rogers Western World was to be built in Orlando as a huge Old West-themed resort with a dude ranch. Governor Haydon Burns pledged his assistance in making the project happen at a press conference with Roy and his wife Dale Evans in early 1965, but it never got off the ground.

Florida Neverlands, Part Two

Many other Florida theme parks and attractions were envisioned to reap tourist dollars. Most were never built, though some did enjoy brief periods of modest operation. They include:

Vedaland, a theme park to be built in Kissimmee and based on magic and transcendtal meditation, was announced by magician in Doug Henning in 1990, who hoped to duplicate the success of Walt Disney World. The entrance would have included a floating pyramid over a huge lake. Henning had said the park would also include a magic flying chariot carrying riders inside the molecular structure of a rose, a ride over a rainbow emerging from mist, tunnels that guests floated through, and buildings that changed color. The core concept was using entertainment to create spiritual enlightenment.

Planned for 450 acres on U.S. Highway 192 in Kissimmee just west of Old Town, the park was the brain-child of Henning and the Maharishi Mahesh Yogi, the guru of transcendental meditation. The estimated cost was one billion dollars.

In 1994, the group got the East Central Florida Regional Planning Council to give their development plan an extension into late 1997. However, with Henning's death in 2000, interest in the park dissipated and today remains just an illusion.

David Copperfield's Underground was a magic restaurant experience proposed for 1996 that was to be located at the front of Disney-MGM Studios and later at Downtown Disney's West Side.

Bible World, a biblical theme park similar to the existing Holy Land Experience was announced in the 1970s for Kissimmee, but never materialized.

Johnny Weismuller's Tropical Wonderland, originally Johnny Weismuller's Tarzan's Jungleland, was planned for Titusville, Florida, in 1970. It was to have electric boat rides, an Old West town (Dodge

City in 1890), a train ride, and of course, lots and lots of animals. The basic park opened in 1959 before Weismuller, who was famous for portraying the character of Tarzan in the movies, even became involved. It closed in 1973 after Weismuller pulled his support supposedly over issues regarding the treatment of the animals. Of course, poor attendance didn't help matters either.

Interama, inspired by the recently opened Disneyland in 1955 and the World's Fairs, was announced in the late 1950s as a permanent international exhibition park to be built in North Miami. Governments of various countries would contribute to the building and staffing of their representative pavilions. Complications in the financing and zoning process haunted the project right into 1985, when its 300 acres were sold to expand Florida International University's Bay Vista Campus.

Little England (at one time called British Kingdom) was the dream of British grocery store magnate Lewis Cartier who saw the huge influx of British tourists to Walt Disney World and so began developing a British-themed park slated for Kissimmee in the early 1980s. Actual building materials, and even buildings, were imported from England to create a small but authentic country village for the first phase, but those English tiles and wood rotted in the hot, humid Florida weather as they awaited the start of construction. The notorious Florida insects took care of whatever the weather didn't destroy.

Xanadu, the home of the future in Kissimmee, was built with polyurethane insulation foam rather than concrete for quick and inexpensive construction. Try to imagine a styrofoam cup turned upside down and the interior filled with an automated system controlled by Commodore computers handling security, an entertainment center, a kitchen (that could be programmed to cook a meal at a future date and time), and even things like fire protection and energy consumption. Xanadu opened in 1983 to take advantage of the interest in the newly opened Epcot Center. It closed in 1996 and was bulldozed in 2005, but, at its peak, it welcomed more than 1,000 guests per day.

Main Street Music 1971

Former Walt Disney World Music Director Jim Christensen stated:

> The challenge was to produce atmosphere groups similar to those at Disneyland that would work in this new environment of Florida.

The local Orlando talent pool in 1971 was unable to supply all the musical entertainers needed, so auditions were held in several cities around the country, including Chicago, New York City, Los Angeles, Las Vegas, and Miami. Many performers did not fully understand the nature and requirements of performing in a Disney theme park and left shortly after being hired.

A 1973 picture disc called *A Musical Souvenir of Walt Disney World's Magic Kingdom* featured the following liner notes about the original musical entertainment on Main Street:

> THE WALT DISNEY WORLD BAND: This band of on-the-go musicians provides Magic Kingdom guests with plenty of Sousa marches, turn-of-the-century oldies, Disney classic favorites, and humorous arrangements of today's top show tunes.

> THE DAPPER DANS: These four "happy men of Main Street" can be found in the shops and on the street corners singing your favorite barbershop melodies.

> THE SAXOPHONE QUARTET: (Keystone Kops) Dressed in nostalgic costumes of the 1920s, these talented saxophonists are ready for a musical chase down Main Street, USA just when you least expect it!

> THE MAIN STREET PIANIST: Whether playing your favorite ragtime tune or leading a sing-along, this piano player is always adding to the happy mood of Walt Disney World's guests.

> THE TOWN BAND: The butcher, the baker, and the candlestick maker all get together for some musical fun in Town Square.

In the earliest years, there were other musical acts like the Fire Department Band and the Crystal Palace Trio as well.

Former Executive Vice President of Walt Disney Entertainment Ron Logan said:

> I was in the Magic Kingdom and heard the Dapper Dans sing live. I felt like I was experiencing it in "real time" but "real time" of the past. It hit me that the Main Street environment must be kept as "live" as it could be. "Live" is part of the "real" environment.

Jim Christensen was brought in from Disneyland to get the Walt Disney World Marching Band started. Unlike Disneyland's 16 piece band, Walt Disney World's had 20 pieces. Christensen's assistant, Stan Freese, took over as the WDW bandleader.

A Disneyland tradition from the Coke Refreshment Corner at the end of Main Street was imported to the Magic Kingdom when it opened and continues to this day at a similar location, Casey's Corner.

The lengthy piano mirror allows the pianist to play and still interact with the guests who can see his face and he can see them. Besides tunes from the time period, the pianist often includes a variety of Disney tunes in addition to corny jokes and banter.

Debuting in 2000, the Main Street Philharmonic was a 12 piece brass-and-percussion ensemble attired in red-and-white uniforms playing in Town Square to create a turn-of-the-century ambience with tunes like "Take Me Out to the Ball Game", "76 Trombones", and "Alexander's Rag Time Band". In particular, they were featured in the nightly flag retreat ceremony. The band is typically part of the pre-entertainment for the afternoon parade on weekdays.

While some people have claimed that Main Street, USA really has no attractions, they forget that Main Street itself is the attraction, and a significant part of all that is its distinctive, optimistic music.

Hurricanes

One of the reasons rarely discussed about why Walt Disney selected the Orlando area for Walt Disney World was that it was far enough up the coast and far enough inland that it would be reasonably safe from Florida's notorious hurricanes and their devastating effects.

For much of its forty-five year history that has been true, with a few notable exceptions.

On August 31, 1985, Walt Disney World closed as early as 5:00pm because of Hurricane Elena. Roughly ten years later, on August 2, 1995, Hurricane Erin resulted in a late opening at the theme parks. Everything opened at 11:00am, although guests endured rain for the rest of the day.

The first time a hurricane was so severe that there were massive closures at Walt Disney World was the arrival of Hurricane Floyd, a category four storm, in September 1999. For the first time in its twenty-eight year history, the theme parks and other attraction areas closed to the general public for over a full day since it was predicted the hurricane would directly strike the area.

As Hurricane Floyd approached on Tuesday September 14, 1999, Disney closed the Magic Kingdom and Epcot at 2:00pm and Disney-MGM Studios, Disney's Animal Kingdom, and the Downtown Disney area and water parks an hour later.

Guests who were staying in low-lying areas like Disney's Fort Wilderness Resort and Campground, and some buildings at Disney's Caribbean Beach Resort and Disney's All-Star Resort were evacuated to Disney's Coronado Springs Resort and Disney's Yacht and Beach Club Resorts because of the possibility of flooding.

These resorts offered accommodations in the convention centers as well as some heavily discounted rooms. At the convention centers, movies were shown on big-screen televisions and cast members coordinated games and crafts.

When Floyd curved away from its predicted path, on September 15, Disney approved the re-opening of Animal Kingdom at noon for resort guests only and Downtown Disney at 4:00pm.

A toy company was holding its convention at Disney's Grand Floridian Resort and Spa during Hurricane Floyd. According to the September 23, 1999, edition of *Eyes and Ears*, the cast member newsletter:

> Conventioneers were so impressed with the way the resort's cast members handled the emergency that they donated all the toys they had to the families of the cast members who were staying at the resort on ride-out crews.

In 2004, WDW closed for hurricanes Charley, Frances, and Jeanne. It opened immediately after each one passed and didn't file a single insurance claim. There were no injuries reported and only minor landscaping and light structural damage, like downed street lights, trees, and signs.

Hurricane Charley closed all four Walt Disney World parks at 1:00pm the day before the storm in August 2004; they reopened late the next afternoon. Because of the animals, DAK never opened at all on the day before the storm. Damage again was minimal, primarily from winds and rain, though there were some uprooted trees.

On September 4, 2004, Hurricane Frances struck and disrupted operation of WDW, closing the parks and water parks for one day. Hurricane Jeanne closed everything again on September 26, 2004. Hurricane Ivan was whirling around at the same time and was charted to effect Disney World, but veered away.

On October 24, 2005, the parks, water parks, Downtown Disney, and Disney's Wide World of Sports closed for a day because of Hurricane Wilma as a precaution, even though the storm was expected to pass about 100 miles south of Walt Disney World property. Again, the fear was of high winds and heavy rain.

In 2009, Walt Disney World earned the storm-ready designation from the National Oceanic and Atmospheric Administration (NOAA), meaning it is one of the safest places in the United States to be when a hurricane strikes.

First Participants

Here is the official 1971 pre-opening list of operating participants:

- Kal Kan Kennel Club will be similar to the facility they sponsor at Disneyland, which is a holding area for the pets of guests visiting Disneyland. The only difference will be over night accommodations for pets in WDW.

- Gulf Oil, in addition to the service stations located on the project for both guests and employees, will sponsor the introduction to the Walt Disney Story which will be located in the Main Street Hotel building on Town Square.

- Oscar Mayer will be billboard sponsor of the Hotel Coffee Shop in Town Square. This will be our prime in-park breakfast area for Walt Disney World. Their ham, sausage, and wieners will be served exclusively in the Hotel Coffee Shop and throughout the theme park.

- GAF Corporation will have an operation similar to their Disneyland facility, dispensing photo information to guests visiting the theme park. They will also provide photo trail signs, which are the picture-taking spots they have selected throughout the park. Their film will be the official film of Walt Disney World, as it is at Disneyland. (In 1970, GAF replaced the longtime Disney participant, Kodak.)

- Savannah Sugar will be in the Market House, and will be the official sugar of Walt Disney World. Their section will include penny candy as was found in turn-of-the-century market houses.

- J.M Smucker will be the second participant in the Market House, and will display and sell gift packs of their jams and jellies. Their products will be served throughout Walt Disney World.

- Planter's nut products will also be featured in the Market House.

- Hallmark will have a shop similar to their facility at Disneyland, which they will operate themselves. We have recently entered into a licensing agreement with Hallmark for use of the Disney characters on cards and other products outside Disneyland.

- The Coca-Cola Company will have two locations within the theme park: Main Street Refreshment Corner and the Tomorrowland Terrace. Their products include Coca-Cola, TAB, Fresca, and Fanta Flavor, and will be served at both locations.

- Sara Lee will sponsor the Main Street Bake Shop, a self-service snack operation. Sara Lee products will be sold exclusively at this location.

- Bordens will sponsor the Ice Cream Parlor and their milk, ice cream, and cheese products will be served and sold exclusively in Walt Disney World. In addition to the Main Street locations, Bordens will have identification on all ice-cream carts, as well as a soft ice-cream stand in Fantasyland.

- Florida Citrus will sponsor the Tiki Room in Walt Disney World. Our contract states that we cannot use anything but Florida Citrus products on the property. Individual brands cannot be promoted, only citrus from Florida.

- Pepsi-Cola and Fritos, because they are the same company (PepsiCo), will have joint sponsorship of the Bear Band. In conjunction with the show, there is an eating facility which will consist of the Mile Long Bar and Pecos Café. Their products will be served exclusively in these locations. In addition to Pepsi-Cola, Diet Pepsi, and Teem, they will also have their flavor line available. Fritos will dominate the snack food area with corn chips, potato chips, and onion rings. Both brands will be served throughout the park.

- Welch Food's products will be served exclusively at the Mickey Mouse Refreshment Stand in Fantasyland. Their only area of exclusivity is grape juice, and this is somewhat restricted throughout the park.

Hidden Handprints at Magic of Disney Animation

On May 1, 1989, Disney-MGM Studios officially opened with a dedication ceremony led by Disney CEO Michael Eisner. However, not long afterwards on that same day, there was another dedication ceremony in front of the Magic of Disney Animation building.

Roy E. Disney talked at a podium set up in the front of the attraction where he emphasized that hand-drawn animation was the focal point of the Disney company. He continued to emphasize that animation was the start of the company and that with the newly opened Disney Feature Animation Studio Florida, "a new day for animation will be dawning". The animated feature film *The Little Mermaid* would debut in November, just six months later, proving Roy correct.

Joining in the dedication were several Disney animators who had made significant contributions to the field: Frank Thomas, Ollie Johnston, Ward Kimball, Marc Davis, Ken O'Connor, and Ken Anderson. O' Connor, who was primarily known for his work on backgrounds in Disney animated films, was there because he had worked as a consultant on the *Back to Neverland* short film being shown in the pavilion.

The one snag in the ceremony was a literal snag as the cover over the elaborate animation film strip sculpture at the front of the building got caught on a pointy outcropping of the sculpture. Amid the fanfare, releasing of balloons, and applause, several Disney executives struggled in a tug-of-war to release the red cover from its entanglement, and eventually succeeded.

There was also a ceremony where these six animation legends put their handprints and autographs into cement blocks to be placed in an alcove of the outdoor animation courtyard inside the building.

The original intention was that there were would be two handprints per block, as demonstrated on the one featuring Frank Thomas and

Ollie Johnston, longtime friends as well as co-workers. Their hands and signatures are neatly and symmetrically imprinted, along with an impression of their pencils. This was how all the blocks were to look.

But another block features three handprints and signatures—Marc Davis, Ken Anderson, and Ken O'Connor—once again with impressions of their drawing pencils. Anderson's signature seems crowded and his last name curves downward as if squeezed for space or an afterthought.

The secret is clear on the final block, with the handprint of the exuberant Ward Kimball, an extrovert known for being an unpredictable maverick. Not only did he make sure his pencil was broken before being imprinted, he also spread his fingers wide so he could make a second impression. Close examination will reveal that he has six fingers on each hand, something that most guests missed at a casual glance.

Also, in a fit of high spirits, he filled the bottom half of the block with a quick drawing of Mickey Mouse's head in the space that was going to be filled by Ken Anderson. Who would be so bold as to wipe out a Mickey Mouse drawing by Ward Kimball? Apparently, no one. So Anderson squeezed in to a space on another block.

Those hidden handprints were available for every DHS guest to enjoy until they were removed when the Star Wars Launch Bay opened on December 1, 2015.

Lawnmower Tree at Fort Wilderness

For several decades, a natural wonder delighted guests who came to Fort Wilderness Resort and Campground. Some guests would seek out this living curiosity to see how it had changed over the intervening time since their last visit. They were always surprised.

Years before Walt Disney World opened, someone who lived in the area had leaned an old, push-style blade lawnmower up against a tree and left it there. No one seems to know who that person was or why they left the lawnmower.

When a tree is growing, and it encounters something that gets in the way of its growth, it can do three things: stop growing, grow away from it, or grow around it. The tree grew through the tool so that it was absorbed and became part of the tree's gnarled roots above the ground, with significant rusting parts sticking out prominently.

As the area was being developed for the campground, the lawnmower tree was discovered by Imagineers who thought it looked interesting and decided to leave it as a hidden treasure rather than remove it.

The tree was located just off the sidewalk about five feet from the path roughly halfway between Pioneer Hall and the marina, about a hundred feet off the lake.

The Imagineers even decided to create a back story to explain its existence and integrate it into the lore of the campground. They installed a sign next to it that read:

> Too long did Billy Bowlegs
> Park his reel slow mower
> Alas, one warm and sunny day
> Aside a real fast grower

The lawnmower tree was a popular landmark at the resort since its opening in November 1971. As the decades passed, however, more and more of the lawnmower disappeared into the tree as it expanded until around 2007 when just a few rusting blades were still visible at the foot of the tree.

By then, the tree was dead, either through natural causes or having most of its upper half cut off. Only about twelve feet of the trunk remained and the tree had stopped absorbing the lawnmower.

Disney Legal determined that the rusty relic posed a possible safety hazard since guests sometimes would go up and touch the parts, and so the company hired an outside contractor to quietly remove the tree in late October 2013 without alerting the guests.

The tree was so well known that it was listed in the earliest Birnbaum Disney World guidebooks as "a point of interest worth hunting down" and continued to be listed until recently.

The Disney company itself promoted the lawnmower tree as a "fun fact" on official handouts to the media and it appeared on the earliest campground maps.

Over the years, many significant landmarks have disappeared from Fort Wilderness including the famous railroad; the first water park, River Country; the petting zoo that had Minnie Moo the cow with the black three-circled Mickey Mouse imprint on her side, and various food trucks.

Osborne Spectacle of Dancing Lights, Part One

Sadly, Christmas 2015 was the last season for the Osborne Spectacle of Dancing Lights at Disney's Hollywood Studios, as the Streets of America were demolished for further expansion construction of the new Star Wars Land. There is always the hope that Disney might consider relocating the beloved lighting display somewhere else.

William Jennings Osborne, who preferred being called Jennings, was born in 1943. With his wife, Mitzi, they founded in 1968 the Arkansas Research Medical Testing Center in Little Rock. Its success enabled them to buy a large estate in the middle of town.

In 1980, they had a daughter named Allison Brianne who went by the nickname Breezy from her middle name, even as she grew into adulthood. Her father was extremely busy with his business and so was not always around. When Breezy was six years old in 1986, he asked her what she wanted for Christmas, expecting some type of popular toy on maybe even a pony.

Breezy replied that she wanted to spend time together with her often-absent dad hanging lights on the outside of the house for the holidays. Jennings realized that he was missing the most important part of his life, spending time with his young daughter. That Christmas, Jennings extravagantly decorated the outside of the house with over a thousand Christmas lights, to the joy of the entire family.

Every year after that, it became a tradition, and Jennings kept adding more and more lights. However, the Jennings home was located on one of the busiest streets in Little Rock and as the fame of this display spread, it resulted in severe traffic problems as visitors clogged the street to view the illuminated spectacle. When neighbors complained, Jennings bought the houses on either side of him and decorated them as well.

The display grew to millions of lights and in 1994 six neighbors filed a lawsuit with the county court that they won and which Jennings appealed to the state supreme court, where he also lost. Jennings' appeal to the United States Supreme Court was denied and he was ordered to no longer operate the magnificent display. Shortly after his loss, in December 1994, he told *The New York Times*:

> I do this to make people happy. It just makes me so sad that a few people could ruin something that so many enjoy. Every day is Christmas to me and I want to take everybody along.

Walt Disney World Executive Vice President Bruce Laval saw the report on CNN and assigned Show Director John Phelan to contact Jennings in the hopes of having an annual Christmas event to match the ones offered at the Magic Kingdom and Epcot.

Jennings and his family were huge Disney fans and an arrangement was made. Jennings never received any money for the use of his lights or his name. His family would usually come down to Walt Disney World for about a week during the end of December and be put up at Disney's expense at the Grand Floridian to visit the parks. The family would come over one night to Disney-MGM Studios where a special ceremony was held for Jennings and his daughter Breezy to turn on the lights that evening.

Jennings passed away from complications of heart surgery at the age of 67 in July 2011.

Even though Jennings was ordered to remove his massive light display on his home, he did continue to decorate the outside of his houses in a much more modest fashion until his death. He and Breezy still hung some of the decorations themselves.

Osborne Spectacle of Dancing Lights, Part Two

The Osborne Spectacle of Dancing Lights was exhibited for twenty Christmases beginning in 1995 at Disney's Hollywood Studios. Over the years, the show has undergone several changes, but here are a few items that guests may have missed over the years.

When the four 18-wheel Mayflower moving vans arrived at Walt Disney World on November 4, 1995, and the lights were unloaded, Show Director John Phelan discovered a figure of a cat with an arched back outlined in purple. Since the display was announced as opening in just three weeks, on November 24, Phelan contacted Jennings Osborne to identify where the cat fit into the overall Christmas display and if it were perhaps a tribute to an Osborne pet. An amused Jennings replied that it was part of his Halloween lighting and he had shipped it by accident. He had three huge backyard storage sheds filled with his holiday lights, so it was easy to make a mistake.

Phelan kept the cat and had it re-lit in a holiday style and added to the display. Each year, the Walt Disney World lighting crew hides it somewhere in the display without letting Phelan know its location, thus making him go and find it. It is in a different place each year.

Also hidden in the lights is a red razorback hog in homage to the University of Arkansas Razorbacks football team. Jennings was a huge Razorbacks fan and hosted free barbecues at games.

In 2006, approximately four hundred dimmer relay and control switches were added to the display so the lights could be choreographed to a musical score. The holiday event, now with more than five million lights, was renamed the Osborne Family Spectacle of *Dancing* Lights.

Disney was not the first to use dancing lights, but its display was the largest. The company continued to update and add more and more lights each year.

One year, special glasses were given away that allowed guests who wore them to see images of angels in the lights. Because of a controversy over the religious aspects of the angels, the glasses were redone the next year so guests could see snowflakes instead. The glasses also worked on your own Christmas tree at home.

The lights for the display were converted to energy-efficient LED lights beginning in 2011, making the lights not only environmentally friendly and less expensive in terms of electricity usage, but also brighter. Scenes and music from the ABC holiday show *Prep & Landing* have also been added.

The infamous "leg lamp" from the popular movie *A Christmas Story* is in one of the windows. Glow with the Show Mickey ears were introduced in 2013. Santa Goofy has been part of the experience for several years as well.

Of course, there are dozens of hidden Mickeys as well, from a toy soldier with mouse ears on his hat to a marking spot on the rear end of a Dalmatian puppy to the more traditional three-circled images in a variety of colors. The Mickey-Mouse-driving-a-train image was part of the original display in Arkansas.

The red canopy of lights once adorned the outdoor driveway of the Osborne home. The canopy was lower when it was on Jennings' street because he wanted people to feel immersed in the lights. He said:

> I like creating memories that people won't soon forget. I want the people to feel like they are inside the lights, looking out at the world.

Whatever Happened to Minnie Moo?

Mickey Moo, a white Holstein cow with a black Mickey Mouse head silhouette shape naturally occurring on her side, was housed in Big Thunder Ranch at Disneyland's Frontierland in 1988. Mickey Moo was a part of Mickey's 60th birthday celebration that year but instantly became a popular attraction for guests.

The unusual marking on the side of the cow was not quite as unusual as it was originally assumed. A Midwest farmer contacted the Disney company with photos of his own cow that had the same type of Mickey Mouse silhouette head.

Minnie Moo, the white Holstein with a similar black Mickey Mouse head silhouette, came to the Walt Disney World Resort from Edgerton, Minnesota, in 1990, living first in the Magic Kingdom.

Grandma Duck's Petting Farm operated at Mickey's Birthdayland/ Mickey's Starland from 1988–1996. In 1996, the area was transformed into the Barnstormer at Goofy's Wise Acres Farm.

With this change, Minnie Moo and the other animals were moved to a petting farm at the Tri-Circle-D Ranch (near the pony rides) in Fort Wilderness Resort and Campground. Minnie Moo died in August 2001, at the age of fifteen, a little more than the average lifespan for a cow.

The Disney company did not release a notice of her death. Disney spokesman John McClintock said that "it was too sensitive" a subject. Disney also never officially revealed to guests that the 400-pound spotted grouper named Orson at Epcot's Living Seas Pavilion went to the big seafood buffet in the sky.

The animals were sequestered in their pens for the health and safety of both the guests and the animals themselves, but were clearly visible. The petting farm was officially closed early in 2005 with the animals relocated to Animal Kingdom's Affection Section.

To debunk a Disney urban myth, there was only one Minnie Moo (and only one Mickey Moo). Many people claim that there were multiple Minnies over the years, but that is not true. When they died, the Disney company did not contemplate replacing them.

It was estimated that millions of adults and children visited Minnie Moo, petted her, talked to her, and took her photo. She was prominently used in publicity material, although she was occasionally confused with Mickey Moo.

A memorial plaque for Minnie Moo was placed on the wall on the right-hand side in the trophy room (now the Walt Disney Horse Museum room) at the barn at Fort Wilderness Resort & Campground but was removed some years ago. Below it were photos of some of the animals at the petting zoo, including goats and "Chester" the pig that have also been removed.

Tom Hopkins, animal operations director at for Disney's Animal Programs, said at the time of Minnie Moo's death from natural causes:

> Minnie Moo brought much joy to both our guests and our cast members. We will miss her greatly.

The popularity of Mickey Moo and Minnie Moo sparked a short-lived frenzy where the Disney company was inundated with offers of various animals that had a Mickey Mouse-type marking on them, from pigs and dogs to even inanimate objects like potatoes.

In January 1991, Walt Disney World purchased an Iowa pig named Mickey from Tom and Teresa Reuter of Monticello that had three linked black spots resembling the silhouette of Mickey Mouse's head. They also took a brother piglet with similar markings.

Mickey Pig and Mickey Piglet joined Minnie Moo. Teresa Reuter said she and her husband wouldn't lose any money by not sending the six month pig to market, where it would have fetched about $130.

The Story of Discovery Island

The Walt Disney Company bought Riles Island in Bay Lake in 1965 along with some surrounding property. Walt intended it to be called Blackbeard's Island to theme in with the movie *Blackbeard's Ghost* (1968), which was filmed in late 1966.

In early 1973, the Disney company announced that the island would be named "Treasure Island" after the 1950 Disney live-action feature film and would have walkways, small lakes, and waterfalls available to "explorers and picnickers". There were plans to build Ben Gunn's fort, the Benbow Inn, and the wreck of the *Hispaniola*, as well as other physical aspects from the film and novel. There would be nearly 600 real and rare tropical birds on the island.

On April 8, 1974, after the Disney company used 15,000 cubic yards of soil and 500 tons of boulders and 500 tons of trees to transform the landscape, Treasure Island opened to the public. It was a sanctuary for numerous birds, reptiles, mammals, and other non-avian species.

There was also a beached ship, but not the *Hispaniola*. It was the remains of Captain Flint's ship, the *Walrus*, according to the original map.

That early Walt Disney World map of the island for guests proclaimed:

> Sail the Seven Seas of Walt Disney World to an island filled with tropic beauty, colorful birds, and the mystery of Ben Gunn's buried treasure!

Cast members wore appropriately themed pirate wardrobe. The names of locations around the island included Jolly Roger Wharf, Buccaneer's Cove, Doubloon Lagoon, Mutineer Falls, Skeleton Island, Black Dog Swamp, Scavenger Beach, Rum Point, and the Mizzen Mast.

The reverse side of the tri-fold map claimed that some of the future attractions would include:

- **Billy Bones's Dilemma**
  Captain Flint's first mate falls prey to the perils of the open sea.
- **The Blockhouse**
  Site of the battle for the treasure map. "Though fully armed …
  we were still out-numbered by Long John Silver's buccaneers!"
- **Spy Glass Hill**
  A fantastic group of rocks in the heart of the island. In this primeval playground, you'll discover the secrets of this treasure isle!
- **Ben Gunn's Cave**
  As mysterious as the strange hermit himself. Its exact location is unknown even today … but we know it's someplace on the island!
- **Wreck of the Hispaniola**
  This seagoing vessel led by Captain Smollet once anchored here in search of buried treasure … only to be overtaken by her mutinous crew, headed by the self-appointed captain, Long John Silver! She was later run ashore by the brave young Jim Hawkins … never to sail again!

In some aspects, the island would resemble a more adult version of the iconic Tom Sawyer Island in the Magic Kingdom with plenty of "natural" wonders to explore, as well as a mystery to be solved.

The island could be accessed for a half-day experience by either taking a direct motor launch from a resort dock or as part of the Walt Disney World Cruise, a tour of the Seven Seas Lagoon and Bay Lake that stopped at the island.

For unknown reasons, the pirate theme was abandoned and the island was renamed yet again, in 1977, to Discovery Island It became an official zoological park accredited by the American Association of Zoos and Aquariums.

Discovery Island closed to the public on April 8, 1999. During the next three months, the wildlife was relocated to Animal Kingdom in a hub area that was rechristened Discovery Island. Disney claimed that lagging attendance, some maintenance issues, and the fact that Animal Kingdom was better equipped to handle the welfare of the animals contributed to the island's closing.

The Vacation Kingdom

Because of its warm weather and rustic natural beauty, Florida was a tourist destination as early as the 19th century when Silver Springs hosted paying visitors in 1860. That site became even more popular when the famous glass-bottom boats were added in 1878.

Attractions like Cypress Gardens (opening in 1936 with gardens, Southern belles, and later water ski shows), Weeki Wachee Springs (opening in 1947 with beautiful live underwater mermaids), Gatorland (opening in 1949 with the opportunity to see alligators up close and personal), and many other smaller roadside attractions were entertainment venues that capitalized on Florida's natural and untamed environment.

No real tourism activity existed in the sleepy little agricultural town of Orlando forty-five years ago. Its commerce consisted mostly of home-town stores and roadside stands to provide the necessities of life. In 1970, Orlando was home to about 90,000 people (according to the census) and was surrounded by orange groves, farms, and wetlands. The main industries in Orlando were cotton, cattle, and citrus fruit.

While the city was growing, it would probably have developed along the lines similar to other mid-size southern cities of today if not for the vision of one man.

As the famous Walt Disney stood on the marshy land in the uncomfortable heat and humidity, he did not see an inhospitable landscape with dangerous swamps hidden in thick forests of tangled trees and scrub brush. Shading his eyes and squinting into the flat distance, Walt saw a city of tomorrow, families enjoying themselves, a towering castle, innovative themed hotels, and much, much more.

No matter how hard the other executives standing next to him squinted or tilted their heads, they couldn't imagine how this unforgiving land could be tamed and twisted to accommodate a magic kingdom, but they were smart enough not to share those negative opinions with Walt.

Even Walt's older brother Roy, who had his doubts, knew that Walt was capable of seeing things that had never been seen and making them real.

Disney landscape designer Bill Evans recalled:

> It was no-good land. It wasn't even good as pastureland. After massive earth-moving we probably had the world's worst soil in which to plant. But if I was fazed for a time, Roy wasn't.

> He had inherited Walt's vision and could see the land down there blossoming into buildings, roads, hills, golf courses, hotels, and all the paraphernalia of a splendid new community. And he wasn't too surprised or downhearted when we had nothing but grief at first.

Walt never cared for sequels. He famously said, "You can't top pigs with pigs" to summarize his experience of releasing three other short cartoons following the extraordinary animated short *The Three Little Pigs* (1933) that featured the same characters but never came close to matching the success or popularity of the original.

It confirmed Walt's belief not to repeat himself with the same thing but to build on that success with something different.

"Walt instinctively resists doing the same thing twice," Roy O. Disney told a reporter. "He likes to try something fresh."

In November 1965, when he finally announced that Disney was coming to Florida, Walt said:

> I've always said that there will never be another Disneyland, and I think it's going to work out that way. But it will be the equivalent of Disneyland. We know the basic things that have family appeal. There are many ways that you can use those certain basic things and give them a new decor, a new treatment. This concept here will have to be something that is unique, so there is a distinction between Disneyland in California and whatever Disney does in Florida.

Imagineer Marvin Davis remembered:

> Walt always steadfastly refused to do another Disneyland because he said he had done the best park he knew how to do and why would he want to repeat himself? He said, 'There are too many things in the world to do that are different and new and more of a challenge to me.' The only reason I'm sure he decided to tackle Disney World was because of its connection to Epcot.

Roy O. Disney's son, Roy Edward Disney, told me:

> Walt wanted to build this futuristic city called Epcot where people were going to live. My dad didn't know how that made us any money. He argued with Walt that we needed to build a Magic Kingdom and some hotels first to get money to afford to build Walt's Epcot.

> Walt kept insisting that Epcot needed to be built first or it would never get built. Walt died while they were having those arguments. So Dad won by default and he regretted winning that way. Walt probably would have been surprised to see what it all is today.

Walt realized that the public wanted some type of entertainment venue similar to Disneyland so that was always part of his plan but just the smallest part tucked away in a corner at the top of the map on the worst land on the property.

Walt's vision was not for just another theme park or even the famous experimental community showcasing new technology but an entire vacation destination. Walt made it clear that the area would be "dedicated to the happiness of the people who live and work and play here".

It would include themed resort hotels, a campground, an airport of the future, an industrial park, a wide variety of land and water recreation facilities including golfing, horseback riding, water skiing, boating, and much more.

"It is the hotels, shops, beaches and other recreational facilities at Walt Disney World that really set the new complex apart," stated *Time* magazine when WDW opened.

Disney publicity in 1971 described it as:

> The Vacation Kingdom of the World. Walt Disney World is a completely new kind of vacation experience. Here you'll find all the fun of California's Disneyland and many new attractions created especially for Walt Disney World. Come for the day...or better yet, plan to stay for your entire vacation!

According to a 1969 Disney publicity release:

> The hotel 'theme resorts'—so called because each is being based upon a single theme that represents a culture or architectural style around the world—will offer far more than simply convenience of location to the new Magic Kingdom and its attractions.

> In design motif, food specialties, recreation activities, convention facilities and even the type of entertainment to be presented, these

major hotels will complement each other and the attractions of the theme park.

Walt Disney World, destined to become a complete family 'Vacation Kingdom,' represents the largest total recreation and entertainment enterprise ever undertaken by a single company.

Walt Disney world's recreation facilities were designed to make your family holiday not only complete but a whole new vacation way of life.

Among the premier recreation attractions of the Vacation Kingdom are two championship golf courses and a myriad of water sports. Best of all, you can play just for fun...or learn to golf or water ski or hit a tennis ball from skilled professionals.

There are plenty of planned and unstructured activities for amateur players and fans including volleyball, shuffleboard, horse shoes, archery, nature hikes, swimming, badminton, croquet, bicycling and special programs for children and youths.

One of the most significant differences was the size of the area. Disneyland covered roughly 160 acres including its parking lot but Walt Disney World encompassed initially over 27,000 acres, twice the size of the island of Manhattan.

In order to manage that area and the construction, a special entity called the Reedy Creek Improvement District was created. Many Disney fans have a vague idea about what that is and what it does, but there seems to be some confusion.

Some have argued that when the Disney company abandoned the idea of Walt's experimental city that the original reason for allowing the company such vast governing power through an improvement district was no longer necessary.

Reedy Creek itself is a natural waterway that runs through the area east of Haines City and enters Disney property west of Celebration and passes between Disney's Animal Kingdom and Blizzard Beach before meandering up near the Magic Kingdom and Bay Lake.

Improvement districts are not unusual but are more often in rural areas needing things like hospitals or fire protection often unavailable in unincorporated sections. There are improvement districts in almost every state in the United States and several in Florida.

Basically, the government has certain responsibilities and duties to people, from providing fire protection, garbage collecting, water and sewer, and street lighting to other services for which people pay taxes. However, sometimes areas need things that are not covered under those general responsiblities, cannot be easily provided, or need to be handled differently.

A specific boundary is established and a district is formed with the approval of a simple majority of the property owners. Once created, the district operates as a political subdivision with a board of directors made up of the propety owners that governs the functions of that district.

These improvement districts can have wide-ranging authority that includes imposing taxes, adopting ordinances, contracing for professional services, constructing and operating improvements, and handling pest control. Overlaps in jurisdiction can and do occur, so coordination is necessary.

Disney aggressively communicates with local, regional, state, and federal regulatory agencies on matters that cross jurisdictional lines.

On May 12, 1967, Florida's then governor Claude Kirk signed a bill into law establishing the Reedy Creek Improvement District (RCID). There were two significant reasons for establishing the Reedy Creek Improvement District.

First, it was to ensure that Florida taxpayers would not be burdened with the cost of providing and maintaining essential public services and infrastructure required to build and operate Walt Disney World. The question was not just how was water and power going to be provided (the nearest high-voltage power line was more than fifteen miles away from WDW property) but more important, who was going to pay for it all? In this way, Disney paid for it all themselves.

Second, since the original plan was to build a community of tomorrow on land encompassing two different counties (Orange and Osceola) that had different standards and regulations, it was necessary to have a unified governing body that could provide the legislative and regulatory flexibility necessary to allow innovative construction techniques, from buildings to roads and water control, as well as environmental protection of the area.

The Walt Disney World property located in Orange County constituted approximately 18,800 acres and in Osceola County approximately 6,200 acres.

The "Epcot Building Codes" that were established are based on a philosophy that encourages new methods in design, construction, and materials. They became "living documents" that served as a valuable reference for other major building codes throughout the

United States and led to a wide range of imaginative projects and ideas such as the construction of a fiberglass castle and an eighteen-story geosphere while assuring a high degree of public safety.

Fiberglass was formerly considered too combustible for structural use. A sophisticated system of sprinklers, computer-controlled smoke detectors, and flame retardants made possible the 189-foot-tall Cinderella Castle that used more fiberglass than any other single structure, up to its construction in 1971.

The first structure built using epoxy glue instead of mortar to reinforce masonry was the Travelodge Hotel on Hotel Plaza Boulevard in Lake Buena Vista in November 1972. It is now the Best Western Lake Buena Vista Resort Hotel.

The first installation in the United States of the Swedish-built automated vacuum assisted collection (AVAC) was for the Magic Kingdom. This unique method of waste collection allows refuse to be deposited at seventeen collection points around the park. Every fifteen minutes it is drawn through twenty-four-inch pneumatic tubes, at speeds up to sixty miles an hour, to a central compactor station at the back of Splash Mountain and then trucked out to waste management.

Disney's Polynesian Village Resort and Contemporary Resort were the first major applications of steel-framed modular construction. Rooms were assembled at a plant six miles away, shipped by truck to the site, and slipped into the framework, with electrical wiring and plumbing already inside.

The Contemporary used an A-frame while the Polynesian utilized stacking. The original design plan for the Polynesian was a pyramid frame that would have made the modular method more necessary.

Tom Moses, the district administrator for the Reedy Creek Improvement District in 1976, stated:

> Of all the innovations at Walt Disney World, the government is probably the most innovative. Our master plan is the one Walt introduced as the company master plan. We update it continually. We say 'no' more than 'yes' to the company. When someone comes with a far-out concept, we say, 'Let's sit down and look at what the regulations say and what you're trying to achieve. Let's see if we can find a way.' We've forced some total changes in design.
>
> One word sums up our codes: flexibility. We believe regulations in most cities are not flexible enough to facilitate the things people want

to do. We were the first to require that there be smoke detectors in lobbies so that an elevator cannot stop on a floor where there's a fire.

We were one of the first to allow for a reduction in fire protection when you put in a sprinkler system. We allow areas in the basement to be screened off instead of walled. They're easier to inspect. We were once the only people to require door closers on hotel rooms. Two other major codes now have this.

We can't get by with anything because there are millions of people out there watching everything we do. People are always writing in to tell us about things. There are a lot of eyes helping us to do our work.

Before Moses came on board as district administrator, he held several related positions including that of building and planning official for Winter Park and technical director of the Southern Building Code Congress.

The RCID requires spinkler systems in all permanent and most temporary buildings, as well as extensive networks of smoke and heat detectors. The systems are monitored by computers which alert the RCID fire department in advance of actual combustion. Response time for the RCID fire department has been consistently clocked at 45 seconds. There are four RCID fire stations, one behind the Magic Kingdom and another behind the mid-point of Epcot's World Showcase.

"We're one of the few fire departments with an ambulance service. We run three ambulances," said Moses. In 1975, the ambulance service responded to 1,800 calls. The fire department responded to 568 calls, 45 of them woods fires and 77 automotive fires.

RCID has spent in excess of a hundred million dollars on public road improvements. Over 167 lane miles of roadways have been funded and maintained without one penny of county, state, or federal funds. RCID also funded the entire cost of traffic controls on State Road 535 when the Crossroads complex opened, even though the intersection was a state road, because it was impacted by traffic from within RCID.

The Vista United Telecommunications system was the first commercial fiber optic system in the United States in 1978 and became a fully digital switching network in 1983. It was the first telephone company in the state of Florida to implement a 911 emergency system.

The Inductive Power Transfer System and Automatic Vehicle Guidance System were the first-of-their kind transportation methods used initially in the Universe of Energy Pavilion at Epcot and The Great Movie Ride at Disney Hollywood Studios.

All of these achievements and many others were the result of having the RCID in place to authorize them.

An improvement district can also have its own law enforcement officers, but Disney felt it was not a wise idea legally or branding-wise to have Disney cast members with loaded guns strapped to their waists wandering through the guest areas.

So, while Disney has hundreds of security officers, arrests and citations are issued by the Florida Highway Patrol along with the Orange County and Osceola County sheriffs' deputies who receive suspects from the Disney security staff. There is a jail cell in the Utilidors under the Magic Kingdom.

RCID has complete jurisdiction over the property owned by the Disney company in central Florida and functions much like a separate county. It provides essential public services to the property such as fire protection, flood control, waste collection, and environmental protection. If it wanted to, the district could build its own airport or nuclear power plant.

RCID receives all its income from taxes and fees imposed within its boundaries. In its 1975 budget of $4,500,000, roughly $4,300,000 came from taxes. The remainder came from interest, fees, and licenses. Not subject to the state limit of ten million dollars on assessed valuation, RCID can tax up to thirty million dollars.

A board of five supervisors elected by the landowners conducts the business of the district. The supervisors must also be landowners. Disney owns the land in the district and since votes are strictly proportional to the acreage owned, the company basically governs its own property.

Disney sells five-acre blocks of undeveloped land to the supervisors and on completion of their terms as supervisor, these individuals sell their land back to the company. The law permits supervisors to vote on contracts between the district and their own companies. The board of directors hold monthly meetings.

There are two incorporated cities within the district. On May 12, 1967, Governor Kirk signed the incorporation acts for two cities: Bay Lake and Reedy Creek. Reedy Creek was renamed as Lake Buena Vista around 1970.

Lake Buena Vista (Mayor Mike Sheehan) and Bay Lake (Mayor Todd Watzel), quietly hidden on property and with security gates, each house roughly two dozen people at any one time. These cities include all the developed land within the property and are populated by Disney employees who pay a low rent. They do not own the land where they live. They elect a city council.

The administration of the district is delegated to a general manager whose responsibilities are similar to those of a typical city manger in Florida.

Donald Greer is the current president of the Board of Supervisors and only the fourth to hold that office since General Joe Potter was elected in 1968. Potter also was the first RCID district administrator. He was succeeded by Tom Moses (1974) and Ray Maxwell (2001). The current district administrator is Bill Warren.

Potter was in charge of preparing the land for construction. (Admiral Joe Fowler was in charge of building on the prepared land.) He supervised the water lines, power lines, communications lines, and roads that went in daily at a fantastic pace in order to meet the announced deadline.

Currently, there are more than three hundred employees of RCID that work at such on-site facilities as a laboratory for testing water and environment concerns, an electric power-generating facility, a water treatment facility, and a recycling center.

RCID is prepared for further expansion. Only 38 percent of available land has been developed at Walt Disney World. Another 2,730 acres are classified as mixed use and available for future development. Approximately 7,940 acres are classified as conservation and permanently set aside for environmental reasons, while another 3,410 acres are wetlands classified as resource management/recreation and are considered inappropriate for development.

RCID created an Environmental Services Department in 1971 and tasked them not to just maintain, but whenever possible, improve the woods, wetlands, and swamps that are native to the property.

The department has its own laboratory where it tests all types of water, including surface water, ground water, potable water, pools, and swim beaches. Soils and sediments also are monitored. The constant environmental monitoring ensures the continuity of water quality within the district.

In essence, RCID is a multi-purpose district that provides essential public services, regulates building codes and land use, institutes environmental protections, and provides direction for the efficient operation of Walt Disney World property.

Disney does have unparalleled control of the property and through RCID is essentially its own government. However, the existence of RCID has allowed for development that would not have been able to be accomplished any other way.

The freedom provided by RCID allowed the property to truly become the vacation destination envisioned by Walt. Visitors spend multiple days and even weeks and are still unable to experience everything that is available.

About the Author

Jim Korkis is an internationally respected Disney historian who has written hundreds of articles and a dozen books about all things Disney over the last thirty-five years.

Jim grew up in Glendale, California, where he was able to meet and interview Walt's original team of animators and Imagineers. In 1995, he relocated to Orlando, Florida, where he worked for Walt Disney World in a variety of capacities, including Entertainment, Animation, Disney Institute, Disney University, College and International Programs, Disney Cruise Line, Disney Design Group, and Marketing.

His original research on Disney history has been used often by the Disney company as well as other organizations such as the Walt Disney Family Museum.

Several websites feature Jim's articles about Disney history:

- MousePlanet.com
- AllEars.net
- Yesterland.com
- CartoonResearch.com
- YourFirstVisit.net

In addition, Jim is a frequent guest on multiple podcasts as well as a consultant and keynote speaker to various businesses and groups.

When Jim worked at Walt Disney World, he was considered a leading expert in WDW history and prepared the questions for the various rounds of the annual cast member WDW trivia competition as well as being the host for the final round.

He wrote quarterly Disney history columns for the *Disney Vacation Club* magazine, the text for WDW trading cards, and often gave presentations and tours to WDW cast members and corporate partners.

Jim is not currently an employee of the Disney company.

To read more stories by Jim Korkis about Disney history, please check out his other books, all available from Theme Park Press.

More Books from Theme Park Press

Theme Park Press is the largest independent publisher of Disney, Disney-related, and general interest theme park books in the world, with dozens of new releases each year.

Our authors include Disney historians like Jim Korkis and Didier Ghez, Disney animators and artists like Mel Shaw and Eric Larson, and such Disney notables as Van France, Tom Nabbe, and Bill "Sully" Sullivan, as well as many promising first-time authors.

We're always looking for new talent.

In March 2016, we published our 100th title. For a complete catalog, including book descriptions and excerpts, please visit:

ThemeParkPress.com

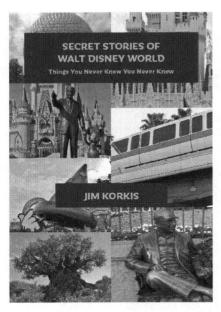

The Rosetta Stone of Disney Magic

Warning! There be secrets ahead. Disney secrets. Mickey doesn't want you to know how the magic is made, but Jim Korkis knows, and if you read Jim's book, you'll know, too. Put the kids to bed. Pull those curtains. Power down that iPhone. Let's keep this just between us...

themeparkpress.com/books/secret-stories-disney-world.htm

Disney History at Its Best

No one knows Disney history, or tells it better, than Jim Korkis, and he's back with a new set of 20 stories from his Vault of Walt. Whether it's Disney films, Disney theme parks, or Walt himself, Jim's stories will charm and delight Disney fans of all ages.

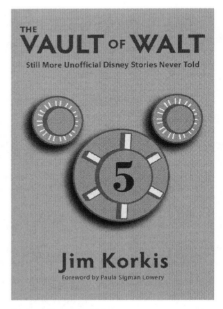

themeparkpress.com/books/vault-walt-5.htm

The Mouse Made EASY

Beat the crowds, the cost, and the chaos, and take the pain out of the pixie dust with Disney experts Dave Shute (yourfirstvisit.net) and Josh Humphrey (easy-wdw.com), whose innovative, step-by-step advice makes the up-to-date easy Guide your indispensable vacation planning partner.

Who's Killing Cast Members?

In this debut novel from former Disney World VIP Tour Guide Annie Salisbury, a body has turned up in the waters of the Jungle Cruise. Wrongfully accused Cast Member Josh Bates must race through the theme parks to solve the murderer's maddening riddles and clear his name.

Welcome, Foolish Readers!

Haunted Mansion expert Jeff Baham recounts the colorful, chilling history of the Mansion and pulls back the shroud on its darkest secrets in this definitive book about Disney's most ghoulish attraction.

themeparkpress.com/books/haunted-mansion.htm

The Story of Walt's EPCOT

Disney historian and urban planner Sam Gennawey traces the evolution of the EPCOT we didn't get and the Epcot we did, in a tour-de-force analysis of Walt's vision for city-building and how his City of Tomorrow might have turned out had he lived.

themeparkpress.com/books/progress-city.htm

Made in the USA
Lexington, KY
12 October 2017